CULTIVATING LIFE

A STORY OF EARTH AND HEARTH

Life on a New Hampshire family farm in the second half of the twentieth century

Helen Coll

© 2001 by Helen Coll. All rights reserved.

No part of this book may be reproduced, stored in a retrieval system, or transmitted by any means, electronic, mechanical, photocopying, recording, or otherwise, without written permission from the author.

ISBN: 0-75966-906-6

This book is printed on acid free paper.

ACKNOWLEDGEMENTS

Thank you to Arlene Garlisi, who first suggested I write a book about the humorous stories of our family life on a farm.

Also thanks in memory of Mea Courinne Duval Taylor, who first sparked in me the desire to know who had farmed here before us.

I am grateful to Bard Rodgers Hamlin, for inspiring me to enroll in Lesley College, obtain my bachelors degree and to write my story. And to George Flavin, my favorite professor at Lesley, who gave me guidance and shepherded the way to accomplish what I thought I could not attain. Their insights illuminated the way.

I am fortunate to have had as editing friends, Alice Bean Brown and Jody Boutwell Saville, and for their skillful and dedicated attention to my manuscript, I am most appreciative.

To Fleur Weymouth, I owe a debt of thanks for her unstinting support, generous heart and faith in my abilities.

And finally, I am eternally grateful to my husband, Archie, for his abiding faith and belief in me and his continuing encouragement to stretch my arms and reach my goals.

This book is dedicated
in love and gratitude
to the following persons
who ALL contributed in creating the person I am today:

to my beloved husband and best friend
Archie

and to our four loving and remarkable children
Suzanne Helen
Mark Richard
Peggy Anne
David Lewis

also to the memory of my adored parents
David Lewis Van Blarcom (1912-1967)
Ruth Woodbury Van Blarcom (1912-1968)

as well as the memory of my cherished grandparents
Willett P. Van Blarcom (1886-1962)
Lulu Lewis Van Blarcom (1884-1978)
Sydney Woodbury (1883-1957)
Florence Elva Rossell Woodbury (1884-1946)

SUNRISE, SUNSET

from "Fiddler On The Roof" lyrics by Sheldon Harnick

Is this the little girl I carried?
Is this the little boy at play?

I don't remember growing older,
When did they?

When did she get to be a beauty?
When did he get to be so tall?

Wasn't it yesterday when they were small?

Sunrise, sunset, sunrise, sunset,
    Swiftly flow the days,
Seedlings opening to sunflowers,
    Blossoming even as we gaze.
Sunrise, sunset, sunrise, sunset,
    Swiftly fly the years,
One season following another,
    Laden with happiness and tears.

What words of wisdom can I give them?
How can I help to ease their way?

Now they must learn from one another,
Day by day.

They look so natural together,
Just like two newly weds should be.

Is there a canopy in store for me?

Sunrise, sunset, sunrise, sunset,
    Swiftly fly the years,
One season following another,
    Laden with happiness and tears.

CONTENTS

	PAGE
FOREWORD by Ronald Jager	xiii
INTRODUCTION by Jody Saville	xv
HISTORICAL PREFACE	xix

CHAPTER ONE	Those Who Came Before	1
CHAPTER TWO	Farming: Beginning a New Way of Life	21
CHAPTER THREE	Knee High by the Fourth of July	26
CHAPTER FOUR	In the Garden	35
CHAPTER FIVE	Calves and Horses, Sheep and Goats, Chickens, Dogs, and Cats	46
CHAPTER SIX	Chickens and More Chickens	60
CHAPTER SEVEN	Rocks, Trees, Birds and Bees	65
CHAPTER EIGHT	Water, Water, Everywhere?	74
CHAPTER NINE	Hazards We Encounter: Animal (Predators) and Human (Vandals)	78
CHAPTER TEN	Farm Hands and Customers' Hands	85
CHAPTER ELEVEN	Eminent Domain	94
CHAPTER TWELVE	The Day I Ran Away	100
CHAPTER THIRTEEN	Family and Home	103
CHAPTER FOURTEEN	And Now...The Rest of the Story	117
CHAPTER FIFTEEN	The Future	138
APPENDIX		146
BIBLIOGRAPHY		161

INDEX OF ILLUSTRATIONS

	PAGE
Map of the Coll farms Today, 2001	xxvii
Jules Duval photos 1899-1919	19
Thelma and Charles Jurva 1936	20
Fannie and Charles Jurva 1950	20
Our Wedding Day—May 3, 1958	25
Old Farm Stand—1969	33
View of all three farms—1998	34
Left: Flower bouquets for sale—1998	45
Below: Helen picking flowers—1996	45
Mark, Peggy, Dave, Suzanne—1969	58
Dave and Mark—1972	58
Peggy and Taffy—1972	59
Suzanne, Cricket, and Dave—1971	59
Archie at pumkin harvest time—1998	84
Helen at corn picking time—1998	84
Rafael Mujica—1976	116
Ileana Wong—1990	116
Ray, Suzanne, Reuben, Ryan—2001	135
Mark, Lori, Joshua—2001	135
Whitney, Lyndsey, Peggy, Paul, Isaac & Abbie—2001	136
Ben, Dave, Kelly, & Emily—2001	136
Helen and Archie Coll—2001	137
Archie Coll Family—2001	137

FOREWORD

A few years ago Helen Coll—her children grown and The Coll Farm and Farm Stand now a thriving family enterprise—paused to take stock of her life. Summoning extraordinary courage, she decided to go back to school, to focus on writing, and eventually to compose a careful account of the life she knew so well: farmer, farmer's wife, mother, businesswoman.

The result is this book, **Cultivating Life,** an aptly titled narrative of a rich life in rural New Hampshire in the last half of the twentieth century. It is a favorable report, there is no doubt about that: unsentimental, tough (sure, they eat some of their animals), full of down-to-earth family stories, and many a verbal snapshot taken from a farmer's wife point of view. There are funny farm stories (the bull in the well), and tales of hard work and long hours, and one remarkable chapter includes a brave and tender account of a wrenching family tragedy.

Farming is a package deal, though, she writes, and "at times it's a love/hate package." Deep into the book she puts it this way: "I love the idea of living on a farm and raising our children here and having the sun shining and the corn growing and hens laying, but I hate it when there hasn't been rain for weeks and storms come and wreck what we have growing and the temperature is 90 in the shade and everything becomes all consuming."

Helen Van Blarcom was a Jaffrey, New Hampshire, farm girl and she married Archie Coll, the farmer son of the farmer across the road and they set out, more than forty years ago, to try to be successful farmers. They had chosen a hard place, for this is a hilly, rocky state, never especially hospitable to farming, and this is a time when fewer and fewer farmers are able to pull it off. They did it—with hens and eggs and corn and a retail farm stand and plenty of calluses and sweat. When she looks back she realizes that they were always cultivating much more than land—land which has changed hand seventeen times since its first clearing, and which will eventually go to their son Mark and his family, and maybe to the next generation after that. They are cultivating life. And the crops are good. In this warm-hearted book family farming is alive and well.

August 2001
Ronald Jager
Washington, New Hampshire

INTRODUCTION

While waiting in the checkout line at a supermarket one day, I overheard the customer ahead of me complaining that a bunch of carrots (rarity in a supermarket) she was buying had dirt on them. She asked the clerk why that was.

"Don't you know how carrots grow?" the clerk asked.

"They just grow on a plant, then you pick them," replied the woman. "So these must have been dropped on the ground."

Doing her best to keep a straight face, the checker patiently explained that carrots grow in the ground with only the green leafy part being visible. To harvest carrots, she continued, one must either pull them out by the tops or loosen the soil with a digging fork first and then pull them out. The customer's face registered total disbelief.

When it was my turn to be checked out, the clerk was still chuckling to herself. I asked if she had had other experiences like the one she just had. Her response was a laugh that really answered my question without further explanation, but she went on to say that incidents like happened all the time. "You would never believe the ideas people have about how produce grows. If you put some in a garden full of vegetables, I think they would likely starve," she concluded.

Even though this incident seemed incredible to me at the time, it has come to mind numerous times while editing the book you hold in your hands. I have not asked her, but author Helen Coll could probably relate dozens of similar experiences with customers over the years.

But why should it be that people are so ignorant about the food they consume? I have asked myself. The answers were not too long in coming. First of all, the vast majority of people in the United States live in urban areas. They have never planted of even seen a productive garden. This country was an agrarian society from its beginnings in the 17th century. It remained an agrarian society well into the 19th century, when the Industrial Revolution began to draw people into the cities to work in the burgeoning factories and industries. Gradually, the small communities nearby began to disappear. Good, productive land began to fall into disuse because the "old folks" were unable to keep up with the work the land demanded. Here in New England evidence abounds that this was once a very different landscape and a different way of life. It is common for hikers in heavily wooded areas to come upon cellar holes of abandoned farms, sometimes even lilacs still growing by what was a doorstep. Taking a plane flight in winter, one can see an astounding number of stone walls that once marked the boundaries of land and fields earlier in the 20th century. As the call of the cities became more attractive, migration continues, until today a family farm is a rarity.

Another reason for the demise of the family farm was the increased demand for food in the more and more densely populated cities. The small farm could not produce the vast amount of food urban areas required, much less process and transport it to where it was needed and be assured of getting it to markets at its peak of freshness and flavor. Therefore, around 1950 a new word appeared in the American vocabulary that in 2001 does not seem new at all—*agribusiness*. It is a far cry from the operation of the small family farm. Agribusiness deals with growing or producing food just as all farms have in centuries past. The differences are in size and scale. These farms, or in some cases co-ops, not only grow or produce food in huge amounts, but they also process, store, and distribute it to the nation's markets. Small farms are unable to compete with such highly organized and powerful operations.

Is it any wonder then that supermarket customers ask about dirt on their carrots? The food they buy is processed, packaged, and transported, sometimes thousands of miles, before consumers see it neatly displayed in attractive plastic packaging at the local supermarket. The result is that few people know how the food they buy got to the bins and shelves of their favorite store.

This book is about a family farm that survived when so many did not. It is in no small way a result of the commitment and dedication of its owners, Archie and Helen Coll, and their willingness to so the strenuous work and put in the long hours necessary to ensure its survival. Because both Archie and Helen had grown up on farms, they knew at the outset what their lives would be like. Nevertheless, they chose to undertake what would be pretty daunting endeavor for most people in order to live the kind of life they wanted and to provide the environment they wanted their children to grow up in. They were convinced that life on the farm would be the best teacher of the values and ideals they hold dear. They were correct. Those who know the now grown Coll children agree that all four have turned out to be the kind of citizens any community would be proud to count among their own.

Life for the Colls was not an idyllic one. As the reader will come to understand, the family faced many problems and crises over the years, including the near loss of the farm through eminent domain. Yet through the story are woven anecdotes about everyday life events and experiences. Often these will make you smile; occasionally they may make you sad. But taken all together, they reveal a cohesive, caring family that came to be through the persistence of parents who believed in what they were doing.

Hard work, long hours, and persistence aside, there is a further aspect to running a successful farm operation that is another strong thread running through this memoir—education. Both Archie and Helen realized their farm could not succeed if they failed to keep up with the times. Therefore, they needed to learn what other farmers were doing to survive. They became members of several farm groups as active participants; Archie even became an officer in some of them while Helen was learning computer skills, budgeting, bookkeeping, and the financial strategies that would keep them afloat. In the process Helen realized her dream of earning a college degree. No mean feat for a woman with such a busy life.

Ultimately the Colls realized that a small farm raising crops for a local market was not going to be a great financial success without some changes. What they did was turn to agribusiness with their egg-producing operation. They learned to use the techniques of production, distribution, and marketing that was proving profitable for other farmers. Thus A & H Farms, Inc. was born. Today their eggs are recognized throughout the Northeast, and egg production is a strong, stable base for their entire farm business. The farm stand on the hill outside Jaffrey, New Hampshire draws customers from all over the Monadnock Region and beyond, and we Jaffreyites count ourselves lucky for it.

We are also lucky that the Colls still grow much of the produce they sell on the land that has been a farm for centuries. Fresher food cannot be found anywhere. There is nothing like corn picked and eaten on the same day. For the convenience of customers, the stand offers fruits and vegetables not grown in New England, and there is a full line of groceries in a town where grocery stores have come and gone, leaving us no choice but to shop in neighboring towns. One cannot help but wonder what those earliest settlers on the Coll land in the 1700s would think if they could see is today. No doubt they would experience culture shock at first, but untimely they would applaud the changes.

Most people will agree that Archie and Helen have made a success of their farm by being willing to adapt and change as times have changed. But it isn't just about change. It is also about what has not changed: the family values, the shared goals, the dedication to hard work, and the vision of the future shared by a young couple early in their marriage. Several times in this book Helen mentions discussions over the dinner table concerning future plans and projects. They learned early on that their thoughts and ideas counted. So what is a family farm anyway? It is a family working together for the benefit of all its members who share common goals, and most of all, love.

Jody Saville

HISTORICAL PREFACE

I feel my life has always had a pastoral painting present in it; I think of a watercolor by Winslow Homer of a Vermont farm. I cannot paint with paints and a brush, but I would like to try to paint with words.

Many years ago, sometime in the 1970s, an older woman came to our farm stand and proceeded to tell me she had been born in our house. That was the beginning of a fascination for me and a yearning to discover who had lived and worked here before us. I was a very busy wife and mother, businesswoman, active in the community and in my church and did not have any time to pursue this allure.

In 1994 I had a health crisis which prompted a change in lifestyle. I was working too obsessively in an atmosphere heavy with tension and stress, which caused a collapse that was manifested by high blood pressure and heart palpitations. From that experience I entered a phase of reflection and contemplation of how to change my life for the better. I rediscovered an earlier goal I had not reached and another aspiration I wanted to work towards; I desired to obtain my Bachelor of Liberal Arts degree, and to write a book about my experience living and working on a family farm in New England in the second half of the twentieth century. I have four children and eight grandchildren and I would like to leave them a memoir of my life so they may have answers to questions, possibly not yet formed, and have a better understanding of me and thus themselves.

Another reason for writing a book about our farm life is to raise social conscience of everyone as to the values of agriculture, both in New England and in America. It is important to preserve a way of life, to protect farmland from further development, and secure the future of farming for the benefit of all citizens. We all eat at least three times a day and the farmers of this country are providing us with that food. There is a saying, "Don't criticize the farmer with your mouth full!"

And so, in the fall of 1996 I enrolled at Lesley University, in the IRO (Intensive Residence Option) program, to obtain my Bachelor of Arts in Liberal Studies, majoring in writing. This was after a schooling hiatus of 39 years. I began my studies by reading several books on writing well in efforts to learn: how to write, what makes good writing, how to get started and keep writing to a finished product, and what makes a good writer.

Why do I want to write? Because I have so many feelings and thoughts and stories to share. I came to a fuller realization of certain elements in my younger life, which have given me a sense of being "freed up" and thus I can move on and now accomplish things I thought I could only dream about, such as graduating from college and writing a memoir.

Through writing this book I hope to tell about a way of life that is almost gone from the New England scene, the working family farm and lifestyle. Only two generations ago, many lived this life, but now very few are left. We are becoming extinct. The passing of time and the loss of this lifestyle are things I think about and hurt about. I am at a point in my life where I feel I am becoming more alive than ever before. I have finally made the time and have the strong desire to write. Part of this "coming alive" was taking the risk of returning to school after so many years.

I began my study of the Indians that roamed our area by reading several books and each resource speaks of the Western Abenaki Indians as the tribe that was most likely in my area of New Hampshire. The name Abenaki means "people of the dawn." The main tribal name is Algonkian (Algonquin), then the Western Abenaki is part of that nation, and the Sokoki are a local tribe under the Abenaki. The Western Abenaki in this area were called the Sokoki, which means "the ones who broke away" or "people who separated." They were a seasonal, nomadic people who made their villages close to a river or lake and to a sizable meadow that would be suitable to grow crops. The town of Jaffrey is just that. It has five lakes/ponds, the Contoocook River (Indian name), and Mt. Monadnock (also Indian, meaning "a mountain that stands alone"). I found this study very interesting and enlightening, and I discovered for myself that they are still here, as part of the citizenry of New Hampshire. They have been largely invisible and have become deprived and dispersed over the years but remain living here in small groups. In *Wisdom's Daughter*, Mitchell, a contributor writes: "It is so sad when people try to homogenize everybody. Everybody be the same. We're just like flowers on the earth. Would be so boring when we go out there and we see nothing but daises, black-and-white daises. Different people, different ideas, and different beliefs, make life so much more interesting" (263). A very beautiful comparison and statement. We need to honor our differences and respect each other.

My next endeavor was to research the settling of Jaffrey, something I was always interested in and had difficulty understanding until I completed my quest. I read two reference books extensively; *History of the Town of Jaffrey, N. H.* by Daniel Cutter, and *History of Jaffrey, Vol. I* by Albert Annett and Alice Lehtinen, along with four other books on Jaffrey.

The settlement happened in two ways and from two directions. One was by soldiers or their descendants who were granted land. They came north from Massachusetts. Another was through the Masonian Proprietors of Portsmouth, New Hampshire. They were speculators and promoters who drew lots of land

and resold them to those settling on them according to specific rules of settlement. They came west from Portsmouth.

1629

The history of the area began in 1629 when Capt. John Mason retained with authority under King James I of England, "for planting, ruling, ordering, and governing of New England in America" (Annett, 29). He obtained the territory now New Hampshire and, "this tract Mason named New Hampshire after his home county of Hampshire, England" (Annett, 30).

1627/28

A year before this grant to Mason, on March 19, 1627/28, without knowledge of Mason, Sir Henry Roswell and associates of Massachusetts were granted, more or less, the same territory. And so there was an overlapping of grants for the same approximate land.

1660

The tanglement of boundary line disputes continued for many years and the settlement of the area was slow. In 1635 Capt. John Mason died and his claim lay idle until 1660 when his grandson, Robert Mason, "secured its affirmation, and made the name of Mason forever inseparable from the history of New Hampshire" (Annett, 32).

It is of some interest here to state that Massachusetts from the beginning of settlement was a Puritan colony, but the Masonian Proprietors generally were closer to the Church of England and they strongly opposed the spread of Massachusetts influence in governmental affairs. Even today we feel the pressure and presence of differences in social thinking and of governmental ideas between New Hampshire and Massachusetts. Our state motto of "Live Free or Die" on our license plates certainly speaks to a strong difference in social conscience. The state as a whole thinks less government is better government.

1665

As a result of the dispute, a petition was taken to the King of England (Charles II) in 1665 by Robert Mason, and after consideration, the Masonian title was confirmed. By this ruling John Mason was granted New Hampshire.

1740

For many, many years the battle continued over the boundary lines between New Hampshire and Massachusetts and was taken to London many different years (1726, 1730, 1732/33, 1737) until finally a decision by the Council of King George II, March 11, 1739/40, decided the line and New Hampshire gained "eight fold" (Annett 39). Among the towns gained was Jaffrey, plus the city of Nashua and twenty other towns. Jaffrey is just over the stateline from Massachusetts by one town, Rindge.

In 1736, a township called Rowley Canada was granted by the Great and General Court of the Province of Massachusetts to officers or soldiers—or their descendants—who had served in the Canada expedition of 1690. Most of the 62 grantees were from Rowley, Massachusetts, or neighboring towns, hence the name Rowley Canada. When laid out, the township included most of what is now Jaffrey and Rindge as well as a small part of Dublin. The townships were called South Monadnock or Monadnock No.1 (now Rindge), Middle Monadnock or Monadnock No. 2 (now Jaffrey), and North Monadnock or Monadnock No. 3 (now Dublin). Little in the way of permanent settlement happened. The Massachusetts General Court willingly granted the townships hoping for a settlement in the great border dispute. This border dispute between Massachusetts and New Hampshire took many years and several court battles before it was ended.

At the same time as the boundary disputes were going on, the great-grandson of Capt. John Mason had come into possession of the Masonian title. He neither liked politics nor legal matters so wanted to sell his grant. The buyers were a company of twelve prominent Portsmouth men to whom he sold his grant for 1500 pounds. These men were educated, resourceful, and had social and governmental connections. They made a judgment to abandon the eastern claim because it was already being settled, and instead turned their interest to the north and west. The land on the border of Massachusetts and New Hampshire, being in dispute, had not much settlement. History now tells us they were generally fair in their dealings with Massachusetts townships. "That an injustice was done to the settlers of Rowley Canada was due to force of circumstance rather than any animosity or injurious intent on the part of the new proprietors" (Annett, 54). To this day I find people very fair in their dealings in this part of the country. I think it and the climate are what keep a lot of people here. We have noticed the differences when traveling and are always happy to come "home." Could the animosity felt so long ago between Massachusetts and New Hampshire still affect us today? Of this I am not sure. Many citizens from Massachusetts retire to New Hampshire, usually for reasons of lower taxes, and then try to bring with them ideals from their former communities. We have many as customers in our farm store and I overhear their discussions from time to time. An example is this: They come to avoid more taxes, but when they get here they want more town facilities, such as better parks, bike paths, and recreational opportunities, but at town meeting vote no on many money issues, especially schooling expenses. I find it very contradictory of them.

1751

One settler I read about was Abel Platts and his son, who had been on the land for ten years. Another was Josiah Ingalls. The ruling was such that they did not have money to pay for the "damages" (cutting trees, clearing land, buildings). Platts was jailed in Portsmouth, but his friends were able to secure his release and he died on his homestead at the age of 91 on August 25, 1817. There may have been other settlers of Rowley Canada, but the records were later lost in a house fire. Platts was probably the first settler and it was said he even stayed on his claim when the Indians were giving trouble and other settlers left. Imagine clearing land, building stone walls, a home, a shed, a barn, thinking all the time this was your land through a grant you were given for military service and then someone (more powerful, wealthy, educated, an entire group of gentlemen!) tells you to pay for the "damages" you have done to their land! Very, very hard to understand and truly feel what Platts must have felt. But in some small way I can. We have had eminent domain experiences three times for a highway, a sewer plant, and a landfill. It is very unpleasant, costly, unnerving, and hurtful.

1749

On June 16, 1749, Joseph Blanchard, acting as agent for the Masonian proprietors, conveyed to 39 associates, "all rights, possession and property" of the Masonian proprietors in the new township of Middle Monadnock (Jaffrey) and they placed themselves under bond until they could make an operative town of 35 square miles of wilderness (Annett, 69). "The towns were not sold out right but were taken into partnership by the grantees and settlers" (Chamberlain, 3). As far as is known, none of the proprietors became residents. They were land developers, not pioneers in for the rough work of homesteading.

The first meeting of the proprietors was January 15, 1749/50. They elected Capt. Peter Powers to survey the townships. (He was the person who drew the lot for our farm, the bulk of Lot 21 Range 6). Each township was divided into lots and ranges. Middle Monadnock (Jaffrey) consisted of 10 ranges, one-half mile wide (E-W) and approximately seven miles in length. The division of these lots and ranges can still be seen in the stone walls that were made as boundaries on farms. Two hundred and twenty lots were laid out of an average of 100 acres in a township of 40 square miles. "Jaffrey began its 'career' in 1749...Spring of 1750 the town had been laid out in so called one-hundred-acre lots on a checkerboard survey, lot lines running generally north and south and range lines generally running east and west. As a matter of fact, the surveying was not very accurate and the lots varied a good deal" (Chamberlain, 3).

1773

Among the Masonian proprietors was the Honorable George Jaffrey III of Portsmouth. He was a member and the clerk of the society and became a member of the Governor's Council. On August 17, 1773, the year the town became incorporated, the town petitioned and was granted the name Jaffrey. As far as anyone knows George Jaffrey never came here. And as far as anyone can tell it is the only Jaffrey in the world. At the time of incorporation there were "303 inhabitants; number of families, 52" (Cutter, 38).

For 24 years the town was known as Middle Monadnock a "more appropriate name...to which by its geographical position it was justly entitled" (Annett, 12). People came and stayed. The forests were cut, fields widened, and buildings were erected. And so it went—for some settlers there was success and a good life for them and their heirs, and for others there was failure. Pioneering was tough. It was a life of hardship and hard work. It is said it had some comforts and enjoyments. They must have come from feelings of accomplishment and closeness of family. It was not easy, but some felt it was a healthy life. It did not give settlers riches but did give them family values. The same is true today for those who are involved in farming. Not many gain riches in wealth but there is satisfaction in living a way of life you choose and raising a family in a way not many can avail themselves of in these times. The settlement of the town went on for many more years. The Meeting House was built (1776), as were churches, schools, farms, stores, and mills. The population has continually increased. The history of the town is always evolving and it is hoped it always will, for when it doesn't a town begins to die.

Who lived and worked on this farm before us? The next step in my inquiry lead me to the Cheshire County Registry of Deeds and to the Cheshire County Probate Court where I researched all the families who preceded us here on this farm.

With the knowledge gained from reading the town histories and the names I learned from the genealogies and narratives, I began with searching through the deeds. I worked backwards to 1799 and possibly the first person who died here, John Wood, and then back from him, with the help of the lot and range numbers of our farm, to the first settler in 1769.

I had waited many years, because of time and work constraints, and finally I was at the place and point of discovering the past history of our home and farm through the lives of those that came before us.

After gathering the names and information from the deeds at the Registry, I then proceeded to the Probate Court to uncover last wills and testaments, auction listings, and inventories of estates. The most exciting single document, all yellowed and brittle from age but still readable, was the eloquently executed last will and testament of John Wood. It was written on July 4, 1799, and he died the next day. In it he expressed his deep religious faith, and very careful and considerate concern for each member of his family (his wife and nine children). Seeing his signature was very exciting for me. He had lived and died here 200 hundred years ago and was a very praiseworthy person. I found myself having to stifle my excitement, for I was in the probate court and it was so quiet and reserved an atmosphere. A thrill, nonetheless, that I relish to this day.

From this experience I learned the value and importance of careful preservation and documentation of personal and civil papers and the need to perform and discharge them. Without them I would not have been able to come to an understanding of their lives and the times they lived in as personally as I now do. I was able to successfully trace seventeen families, and some I really came to know very intimately because of the amount of material available on them. I gained a better understanding of what life was like for them on this farm, how many animals and of what species, taxes paid, values assessed, properties owned, and who was born here and died here.

Our farm has had many owners over the years, unlike some that remain in the same family for generations. Those multi-generational farms I have found to be in the minority. Having so many owners, as ours has, has made my research more difficult but more interesting. Our country's history happened one year at a time and so did the history of our farm. I found relating their time of living here to what was happening elsewhere, to be informative and introspective. The insight into their daily lives I found can be enhanced by knowing the history of the time. Although news in the early days was very slow, eventually they received news, and it must have had impact on their lives.

I had the utmost pleasure of interviewing three people who actually lived and worked this farm, and I viewed old pictures of what the place looked like years ago. The real stories, the personalities, and the pictures intensified my understanding of, and pleasure in, this all-encompassing undertaking.

Charles and Fannie Jurva lived here from 1921 until 1954 and their youngest daughter Thelma was born here. The oldest daughter, Toini, has come to visit every couple of years, and we have enjoyed knowing her and talking with her about her life. She lived and worked as a chiropractor in St. Albans, Vermont, for many years, and at present lives in West Palm Beach, Florida. She is always drawn back to Jaffrey and the farm, and I think a part of her still thinks of this as "her farm." She was here the summer of 1998 and went into the fields to visit Archie and into the farm store, where she proceeded to talk with customers and tell them this was her farm years ago. I interviewed her for my book, as I also interviewed her sister, Thelma, and a worker, Norman, who lived here when they did. I was able to get Toini and Norman together one evening in summer for a marvelously long overdue visit at our dining room table for dessert. They enjoyed talking and I enjoyed listening and learning about how it was for them to live here. It was very touching to see them complimenting each other and listening to another's story and relating to it.

I had previously interviewed Norman and had a wonderful time getting to know him and hearing stories of his experiences, both here and before he lived here. He enjoyed seeing the house once again and looking in the garage where he had signed his name so many years ago. There were some discrepancies between Toini and Norman, but they each experienced life from their own perspectives. Norman said Fannie (the wife and mother) was very good at milking the cows, and that in Finland (where she was born) women did all the milking, but, Toini said, "My mother would not touch the tit of a cow!" Another example of a different recollection was: Toini and her sister Thelma both said their mother liked to bake and was a good baker, but Norman said she bought her baked goods. Never mind; it just is not that important.

Interviewing Norman, Thelma, and Toini was like having the history come to life. Thelma sent me many wonderful pictures taken of her parents, the barn, the house, and my favorite one of her father and she plowing with their horse in the field across the driveway of our farmhouse. Thelma who lived in Holden, Massachusetts, recently died. I am so happy to have had the chance of meeting her and interviewing her. She wrote a delightful letter to me which is in my book.

I know living relatives of another family, Jules and Roseanna Duval, who lived here from 1899 to 1920. Their grandson, Melvin, graduated from high school with Archie and me and now once again lives in Jaffrey. His wife brought me old pictures they have of the farm. I was able to talk with another grandchild, Eleanor, who told me of her grandfather's love of roses. We have an old rose bush in the garden that he may have planted. Jules, I was told by someone at one point in time, worked as a blacksmith out of what is now our garage, and over the years we have found many horseshoes of varying sizes, many of which now hang from our kitchen beam ceiling.

This is the final culmination of the chronology of the families that preceded us on this farm we love so well and now the book begins.

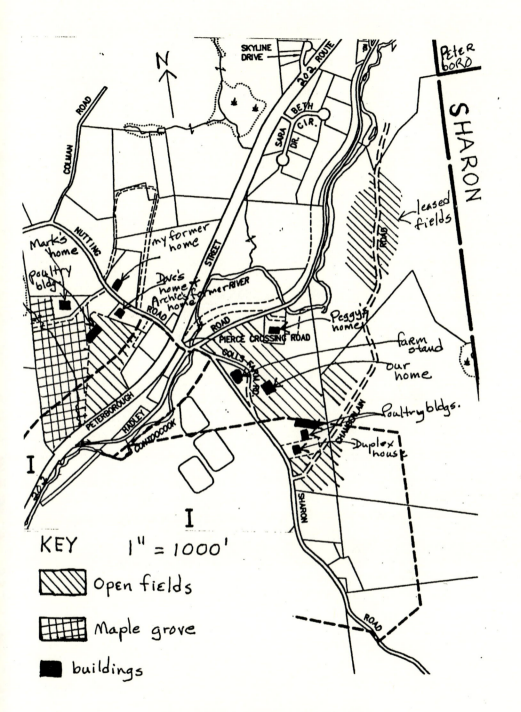

Map of the Coll farms Today, 2001

CULTIVATING LIFE

A STORY OF EARTH AND HEARTH

CHAPTER ONE

THOSE WHO CAME BEFORE

One generation passeth away, and another generation cometh; but the earth abideth forever.
                                                                Ecclesiastes 1:4

    The sun rose about quarter past five with a haze over the land that foretold a sultry summer day. In the two-room with a loft, Cape-style farmhouse, John Wood was seriously ill and preparing for his last day on this mortal earth in which he would serve God and his precious family. It was the Fourth of July, 1799.
    Eben, 21, and John, 25, well-beloved sons of John and Sara were up with the sun and out doing the morning chores. Their minds were on their work but also back in the farmhouse with their father, mother, sisters, and brothers. But there were cows to milk and feed and put out to pasture for the day, and there were the chickens to feed and eggs to gather, as well as sheep to care for, and the sow with eight piglets. They were all growing fast and would be ready for slaughter by fall. When the first chores of the day were done the brothers went back to the house for a hearty breakfast of sausage and eggs and dark, coarse bread.
    Their sisters, Sally, 29, Hepsibath, 27, and Miriam, 22, were busy with the meal preparations. Today Sally was also busy helping her mother to care for her father. Usually the girls would be laughing and enjoying their chores of cooking and washing, but today was different. There was a foreboding silence instead of the daily noise that usually filled each day as they saw to the meals and work in the fields. It was necessary for everyone to help out, offering their hands and backs to whatever chore needed to be done. Each day required a different job. The women did washing one day, baking another, cleaning, spinning, weaving, and gardening. The chores were endless.
    In the springtime Eben and John had seen to the plowing and planting. They used an ox and a wooden plow to turn the soil and then planted the Indian corn, rye, or wheat for fall harvest. And now the crops were growing well, thanks to the abundant rainfall in the spring. It was so very important to have good crops for that was what kept their valuable animals alive all the long, cold winter and the family as well. Now that summer was on, the haying needed to be done. It called for everyone to help, for they had to cut the grass with hand scythes and then turn it with pitchforks until it was completely dry, then load it onto a cart

and bring it to the barn for storage. Rain was the dread when the grass was cut. Everyone hoped for hot, dry weather to get the haying done. The cutting, turning, loading, and unloading was all done in the heat of the day.

The younger brothers, Kimball, 16, and Jere, 14, and Daniel, 9, were expected to work along with their older brothers and sisters to provide for the family. Schooling for the children was done at home by their parents (but soon afterward schoolhouse No. 8 was built at the bottom of the hill below the farm). The Holy Bible and a primer were the only books they had, but reading and writing and arithmetic were important to succeeding in life; Sara and John took the valuable time to see that their children learned what they would need to live productive lives.

The apprehensive atmosphere of the home was heartfelt by everyone. Great sadness pervaded everyone's mind and their hearts and souls. Sara was seeing to her dear husband's needs and comfort as best she could. John called for his son Jere to ride to town (two miles) to summon Roger Gilmore, Joseph Mace, and Nathan Chamberlain to come and make his last will and testament and witness the same, for he was failing fast and wanted to see to his family while he still was able. He praised God for his life, saying, "Thanks be given to God, I here call unto mind the mortality of my body, and knowing that it is appointed for all men to die, do make and ordain this my last will and testament, that is today principally and first of all, I give and recommend my soul unto the hands of God that gave it, and body I recommend it to the earth, to be buried in a Christian-like and decent manner at the discretion of my Executor hereafter named." Then he carefully, meticulously, saw to the every need of his beloved wife Sara and to each of his children, taking into consideration their age and their sex. To his wife he left a room in the house plus cellar room, and provisions for food, clothing, medical care, and a Christian burial. A more touching will I have never read. A man to praise.

John made it through the night but died the following day. The cause of death at age 55 is unknown. His family mourned him greatly and gave him a fine Christian service in the church (Meeting House) where he'd been a founding member. His remains were laid to rest in the Old Burying House, lot number 548 behind the church, where today his gravestone can still be seen. The following quote is on his gravestone:

> "There is a song which doth belong to all the human race,
> Concerning death who steals the breath and bless a comely face.
> Come listen all unto my call which I do make this day,
> For you must die as well as I and pass from hence away."
> It is right next to the building. May God have mercy on him.

*Cultivating Life
A Story of Earth and Hearth*

In the town of Jaffrey, New Hampshire, at present a community of approximately 5,500 residents, there is a farm located two miles north of the Main Street on US Route 202 (see map at the front and back of this book). It has always been a farm since the settling of the town. This is the story of that farm and the people who lived here. Jaffrey has Lake Contoocook, Thorndike Pond, Gilmore Pond, and several other smaller ponds, and the Contoocook River, named by the Indians, meaning: "the pine river from the place of many falls." Our farm is located on either side of the Contoocook River and Route 202 highway.

✿

On this land where we live and work, many people have farmed before us. From 1750 to 1960, 18 families lived here and worked this land (Refer to Appendix p1). Who were they? How did they live? Who was born here, died here? How are we the same? Different? What was this farm like? What can we learn from those who lived here before us?

✿

Before the town was established, the Western Abenaki Indians of the Algonquin tribe roamed this territory. The Western Abenaki in this area were called Sokoki, which means "the one who broke away" or "people who separated." They were a seasonal, nomadic people who located their villages close to a river or lake and to a sizable meadow, which would be suitable to grow crops. We also have Mount Monadnock in our town and the Abenaki looked to mountains for spiritual life. The Abenaki had a spiritual respect for their natural surroundings—the forests and the lakes and rivers that sustained them. They had a very sensitive understanding of the ecosystem because of their continuous involvement with it and observation of it. We are only now, 350 years later, beginning to rediscover what they knew all along.

Legend has it that Mount Monadnock was named by the Indians. The name has many meanings, but the most common and accepted one is: "a mountain that stands alone." The summit of Monadnock is the only point in New England where, on a clear day, all six New England states can be seen. It rises 3,165 feet above sea level.

The Abenaki were dispossessed and have been largely invisible over the intervening years, but they remain here, living in their homeland, scattered in small bands. This is evident in the formation of the Abenaki Indian Center, Chestnut Street, Manchester, New Hampshire, and the Tribal Council at Swanton, Vermont, organized as the Sokoki-St. Francis Nation. Each year there is the Monadnock Valley Indian Festival Pow-Wow held in nearby Keene, New Hampshire. They are living among us but are an invisible people. But more and more people are seeking their "roots" and taking pride in their ancestry and traditions. With all the genealogical information and the Internet available, we may well begin to know them, love them, respect them, and learn from them, for they have endured so much for so many years. We need to honor and respect each other.

✿

The colonial settling of Jaffrey happened in two ways and from two directions. One was by soldiers or their descendants, who were granted parcels of land by the Massachusetts government for their military service in the Canadian expedition of 1690. They came north from Massachusetts. Another was through the Masonian Proprietors of Portsmouth, New Hampshire, who were speculators and promoters; they drew lots and resold them to those settling the land according to specific rules of settlement. They came west from Portsmouth. As far as is known, none of the proprietors became residents. They were land developers, not pioneers interested in the rough work of homesteading. The Honorable George Jaffrey III was one of the proprietors, and in 1773 the town became incorporated and petitioned and was granted the name Jaffrey. It is the only Jaffrey in the world as far anyone knows. At that time there were 303 inhabitants, with 52 families living here. Earlier, Jaffrey was called Rowley Canada by the soldiers who were granted land here and came from Rowley, Massachusetts. Following that it was called Middle Monadnock or Monadnock No. 2, and finally Jaffrey.

Jaffrey is located in the heart of New England in an area called the Monadnock Region. It comprises the southwestern corner of New Hampshire and contains 220,000 acres, 1,000 of which are covered with water and 3,200 of which lie on the mountain. It began its existence as an agricultural community, and then the mills were built on the Contoocook River and industry became predominant. Town historian Alice E. E. Lehtinen once told me that in 1933 Jaffrey had 33 farms. Today it has one commercial farm (ours) and a few smaller farms. As with most New England towns, agriculture is almost a bygone vocation and lifestyle.

✿

It is believed that John Swan was the pioneer who possibly first settled on this farm in 1763. The next person I traced through deed was Aaron Colman, husbandman (a title for a farmer or tiller of the soil), who acquired the land in

1792. At the time of his ownership George Washington was president (1789-1797). On June 21, 1788, New Hampshire ratified the Constitution and became the ninth state in the Union. Aaron sold the farm to Enoch Wellington in 1793. Enoch was from Waltham, Massachusttes. When his first wife died leaving three children, he married Nellie Colman, daughter of Aaron (former owner), and they had two daughters, Abigail and Charlotte. Charlotte was born on this farm. Abigail married Daniel Wood, son of John and Sarah Wood, the next owners, the family described at the beginning of the chapter. Enoch's second wife Nellie died, and he took a third wife, Sarah (Sally) Wood, daughter of John and Sarah Wood; same family again. They had four children. Marrying between neighboring families was very common back then, for there were not a lot of prospective people to choose from, and it was convenient not to have to court from a long distance. In 1799 Enoch sold (or exchanged) the farm to his neighbor John Wood.

✿

When Enoch Wellington died in 1817, in order to settle his estate an auction took place. (Refer to Appendix pp. 6-9.) Everything from pillow cases to pantaloons, furniture to equipment to livestock was sold. Among the persons listed as purchasers were: Luke Wellington, son of Enoch; John Wood and Jonathan Wood sons of John and Sara Wood; future owners Laban Ripley and his son John Ripley; future owner David Chamberlain; Jonas Pierce, the father of a future owner; and neighboring farmers the Nuttings, the Pierces, and the Cutters.

Attending the auction must have been heartwrenching for his family. Thomas, the oldest, was 31 at the time; his sister Abigail was married, as were Sally and Harriet, and Luke at 16 was listed as the purchaser of his father's gold snuff box for $2.00, one pair pantaloons for $2.00, one waistcoat for $1.00, and a pewter plate for 15 cents. Luke went on to be a physician and lived first in New York State and then in Michigan, where he died at age 75. He had nine children. I can just feel the almost palpable emotions on that auction day, when everything, all the family's possessions, had to be auctioned to pay off the estate of a man who had pioneered, worked so hard, and tried to do the best by his family and his town. Now he had died and all had to be sold to settle his debts. People stood by and watched. Some of them were able to bid on some of the things—I cannot understand or begin to fathom what it felt like to be there and see everything of yours put up for auction.

On our farm, which my grandfather Sydney Woodbury originally bought from Charles Jurva and then willed to my mother, there was an auction after he died, which I did attend, of the furniture he had brought up from New Jersey to furnish the farmhouse. It wasn't his personal furniture but some he had bought to furnish the house. It was a public auction. I remember someone wanting to buy the kitchen door right off the house! It had a very special etched glass for the window with a scene of palm trees and a grass hut, and of course it was very old. My father said, "NO, put the door back on the house!" Years later, I was refinishing that same door and I accidentally broke the valuable glass. My husband said he was happy I had broken it and not him, for he would never hear the end of it. I still feel sad when I think about it.

I do not like auctions. I cannot stand a public auction. I don't like someone gaining at another's loss. On the other hand, auctions are necessary to pay the debts. People are able to purchase items they need for their living and usually at a good price. When my father was in fear of my mother's dying (she had cancer for several years), and the farm became too burdensome for him to operate as he had, he decided to have an auction to sell the cows and the equipment. I could not bring myself to attend the auction; I stayed at home on our farm. It was just too sad to see all the cows we knew by name being sold. But he needed the money. I do remember his feeling satisfied with the money they received.

It wasn't long after that my father died—not my mother, who had been terminally ill for six years, but my father. Then she died, 13 days short of a year after his death. Both were 55 years old. Many, many times this happens—one spouse follows the other in death, especially in farm families. I think that when a woman and a man have worked so closely and lived each day totally together, neither one can bear to live for long without the other.

All the people who come to these auctions generally are neighbors and friends and family of the deceased. I know in the case of my father's auction there were neighboring farmers who came to purchase cows and equipment they needed. I remember hearing about one farmer who paid a high price for some plows. He didn't really need the plows, but it was his way of helping out my father. That always endeared him to me. You purchase something of your neighbor's, who no longer lives among you, be it a tablecloth, a coverlet, a pair of boots, a cow, and now it is yours. You use it and think of the one who is gone and it is a way for you to help out the family, to share their life and grief, but yet in another way, it is taking from his family. Oh, the irony of it all.

On the list of the auction of Enoch Wellington all the bidders were men. I wonder if women were allowed to attend and bid? Can't you picture a man bidding on something he thinks his wife might need or like and bringing it home to her. While he was at the auction, she has been home working the farmstead and watching the children, perhaps wondering what he will return with and if he will spend more than they can afford. She is wondering, what will he return home with or how much money will he spend, maybe money they do not have to spare. I can see them when they get to auctioning off the pantaloons and they vary in price from $2.00 way down to 12 cents. Can't you visualize someone holding them up, one at a time, and giving a description? One might be made of wool and have a hole in the rear. This would bring great relief to the tension of the day because laughter would ensue when the auctioneer would say, "And one pair of pantaloons with a large hole in the rear...what do you bid?"

✧

The next owner of the farm was John Wood, the praiseworthy man whose death at 55 I described at the start of the chapter. After his death his family continued to live on the farmstead for 15 more years then moved to New York.

On June 27, 1799, Enoch Wellington sold "21 3/4 acres in the south end of the lot with the buildings to John Wood, from whom he bought at the same time 28 acres in the north east corner of lot 20, range 5, with buildings thereon. This transaction was apparently an exchange of that part of their farms containing the buildings, to the convenience of both parties" (Annett, II, p. 839; Cutter, pp. 521-2; Registry Vol. 32/328). In other words, they switched homes, which were approximately one mile apart. Why they did this is not known, but I speculate it was because John knew he was dying and he wanted his family to live closer to the town. Maybe it was an easier farm for them to operate. This I find so interesting because we now farm both of these farms. One we own and live on, the other we lease as open land from Mrs. Bross for growing sweet corn, there being no buildings left (fire destroyed them in the 1960s). And so, John Wood became a resident on this farm and Enoch moved to the farm we lease. Annett says of John Wood in the *History of Jaffrey, Vol. II:*

> "A man of quiet habits made his will...and although his signature indicates extreme weakness, it is a poignant expression of his careful concern for his family; his sense of justice for all concerned; and his deep religious faith. He lived in an era of Arcadian simplicity ending early in the 19th century, when the New England homestead was the self-sufficient unit of social life, a condition into which his will gives intimate glimpses in its provision for the future welfare of his wife and children. He died the next day...age 55" (866-7). (See the Text of John Wood's will in Appendix, pp. 4-5.)

John Wood was born in Lunenburg, Massachusetts, on February 2, 1743, and he married in Fitchburg, Massachusetts, Sarah Thurston of Fitchburg on Nov. 24, 1767. He came to Jaffrey in 1780, when he was 37. John and Sarah are listed as members of the first church in Jaffrey at its incorporation on May 18, 1780. He is also listed on the earliest tax record of Jaffrey in 1793 along with Aaron Colman:

Wood for ₤2 and Colman for ₤1. When John Wood lived on the neighboring farm George Washington was president, and when he lived here, John Adams was in office. The USS *Constitution* "Old Ironsides" was launched in Boston Harbor on Sept. 20, 1797.

John and Sarah had 11 children: Jonathan, b. 12-4-1768; Sarah (Sally), b. 11-25-70 (married Enoch Wellington); Hepsibath, b. 9-27-1772; John, b. 7-31-1774 d. young; John, 3-9-1777; Miriam, b.3-9-1777 (twin); Ebenezer, b. date unknown; Kimball, b. 1783; Jeremiah, b. date unknown; Daniel, b. about 1790 (married Abigail M. Wellington); and a son born and died 10-10-1792.

Sally Wood became the third wife of Enoch Wellington, and her brother Daniel later married Enoch's daughter, Abigail; siblings marrying two generations of Wellingtons. This previously happened in the history of the farm when Enoch married Nellie Colman, the daughter of previous owner, Aaron Colman. Many times there was marriage between neighboring families, for where else could they find someone they knew so well and that lived close by to court.

As I mentioned earlier, it was very common for neighboring families to intermarry, probably due to difficult travel, lack of time, and slim chances of meeting other eligible people. Also I think it is because neighbors knew each other so well. My husband lived across the road on a neighboring farm (which we now own and operate), when we married in 1958. I remember the newspaper heading for our wedding announcement stating: "Neighboring Farm Families Join For A Spring Wedding." Likewise, Archie's mother as a young girl had lived on the same farm (she was born on the farm) where I lived as a teenager. Just as Archie had lived across the road from me (in the house where he was born), his father was across the road from her when they married in 1935. I have often wondered if Archie's parents got to know each other in some of the same ways that Archie and I did. I was often at his farm playing with his sister, Betty, as well as visiting his mother; also Archie and I were in the same grade at school. There is comfort and security in marrying someone you know so well. Many times people will return to their hometown or high school or college to marry someone they know very well even though they have lived and traveled elsewhere.

✿

In December 1812 Laban Ripley bought this farm from the Wood family. At the time, James Madison was president and the War of 1812 had begun on June 18 against Great Britain. New England opposed the war, but the West favored it. Laban was born November 13, 1758, the 9th. child of Noah and Lydia Ripley, who had nineteen children, seventeen of whom reached maturity. Laban had

Cultivating Life
A Story of Earth and Hearth

married Nancy Stone in Concord, Massachusetts, Sept. 19, 1793. He came to Jaffrey sometime before 1784 for he was listed as a member of the Jaffrey Training Band in that year. The Training Band was a military band of soldiers who met to perform military exercises and prepare to fight if the need arose. I found records in the town library vault of soldiers' compensations for various battles. In 1805 he was agent for schoolhouse No. 8 (formerly located at the base of the hill of our farm) and served as highway surveyor. As a very young man he had been a Revolutionary soldier. Laban and Nancy had three children: Eliza, b. about 1795, died in Jaffrey at age 80; John Stone, b. Feb. 15, 1801, d. Jan. 24, 1827; and Nancy. Eliza and Nancy were both well known schoolteachers. Laban died March 31, 1840, and is buried in the Old Jaffrey Center Burying Yard, grave stone No. 339. And so the picture of Laban is one of a soldier, active town citizen, farmer, and family man.

✿

Daniel and Marietta French lived here from 1846-1855, nine years. The histories do not have their genealogies, and although there were a number of French families in Jaffrey, they were not among them. The records I found were through tracing the deeds and the probating of Daniel's estate and his will. I do not know when or where the Frenches were born, but I do know he died here. Also unknown are their children, if they had any. Daniel lived here before the tax records began and so I do not know the values of their land and buildings at that time. The information from the inventory of Daniel's estate, dated March 2, 1858, tells me he had two pairs of oxen, one black and one red, one cow, one horse, and one colt. He was involved in lumber as he had the tools and wagon for that industry. He in all probability maintained a self-sufficient farm for the family's food and clothing and worked the woodlot for cash and trade. It was a fairly substantial estate. Their food was typical of the times: pork, sausage, hams, beef, dried apples, cider, vinegar, potatoes, butter, and maple syrup. The fact that he owned a covered carriage valued at $23.00 tells me he was fairly wealthy. Judging from the furniture listing, the family had the size house we presently have, complete with window curtains. The deed stated he purchased 120 aces for the sum of $1,200.00 in 1855 from John Cummings. It is not known what happened to Marietta after Daniel's death.

✿

Samuel and Catharine Taggart purchased this farm from John Cummings in 1861, and both of their names appear on the deed, the earliest one I found to have the wife's name on it. I was not able to find any genealogy on them either. The only records were the town tax reports 1861-1864, which stated the value of the land and livestock to be an average of $1,444.00, and the livestock consisted of eight cows and one horse. The fact they had eight cows tells me they were producing milk to sell or trade with neighbors, probably in the town. While they lived here, Abraham Lincoln was president and the Civil War was ongoing. At this time many farm families from Jaffrey were heading westward to settle in New York state and beyond. Lincoln gave his Gettysburg Address on Nov. 19, 1863. I like to think these important events were conversation for Samuel and Catharine and their families and friends. It makes me wonder what they knew of them and how they felt about them.

✧

Dexter Pierce was born, September 4, 1827, on his family farm, which is the same farm my husband Archie was born on in 1938. At the time the Pierces owned it, they also owned the farm across the river, our home farm today. The farms were linked in the early 19th century, and they are linked once again today since Archie and I own and farm them both. One is on one side of Route 202 and the other on the opposite side. They are separated by the Contoocook River and Route 202 and at one time the railroad. But the farms are closer than that sounds; each perches on the hillside opposite the other with Route 202 in the valley between them. By foot the distance between them, walking down one hillside and up the other, is about a quarter mile; even less is the distance a bird would fly. The Pierce family in later years, 1870 to 1930, also owned one or both of the farms. Jonas Pierce (born 1788, died 1857) came to Jaffrey in 1811 and was a prosperous farmer. It is said "his children inherited the spirit of enterprise of their father and became prominent in Jaffrey" (Annett, p. 589). He and his wife Lucinda Bailey had 9 children. Three of their sons—Addison, Benjamin, and Dexter—were farmers on our two farms: Benjamin lived on our home farm and then later Dexter on the same farm, while Addison lived and farmed across the highway after his father Jonas, and he was followed by his son Clark Myron Pierce. (It was Clark Pierce who sold the farm to Archie's father in 1930.) They were all known as public-spirited citizens. Benjamin was selectman in 1868 (.48 Annett). When Dexter and his family lived here, Ulysses S. Grant was president. In 1873 the banks failed and a five-year depression began. When I did the comparison of property (1818-1875, See Appendix p. 2) I wondered why values had not changed much. They could reflect the depression (1873-77), or they just were of less value at that time.

Dexter and his wife Mary E. Buswell had eight children. The three oldest were sons, Jonas Minot, Loren D., and William B., and they inherited this farm that we now live on. Although Dexter was born on the farm of Archie's father, he lived and worked on our home farm until he died, making him a lifelong resident of Jaffrey. In his early business life, which transpired in town, he was engaged with the manufacture of wooden boxes and other woodenware until a fire on June 28, 1868, at A.M. destroyed his mill and box shop. Later he removed to this farm (Was it because of the fire and loss was too great?) which was previously owned, for a short period of time, by his brother Benjamin. Did Benjamin sell to his brother because Benjamin was now a selectman and living in the village? In the library vault papers I found a list of the active members of the East Jaffrey Fire Company for 1863; number 12 on the list was Dexter Pierce. Imagine, Dexter was on the fire company and probably was called to fight the fire at his own mill. Then, because of the total destruction, he moved to his brother's farm which he soon purchased. The road and the railroad crossing at the bottom of the hill are called Pierce's Crossing after this family who farmed and lived on one or both sides for a total of 119 years (1811-1930).

I found an interesting narrative about Dexter's young son Austin: "March 1875, after the completion of the Monadnock Railroad, Austin O. Pierce, a boy about eleven years old, son of Dexter Pierce, who lived on the present Jurva place east of Pierce's Crossing, was riding an untrained colt, which, frightened by the train at the point where the old highway ran side by side north of Cheshire Factory, became unmanageable and with its rider was struck by the engine on a crossing now abandoned and thrown many feet. The colt was so badly mangled that it was immediately killed to relieve its suffering. The boy, miraculously unhurt, sprang to his feet, his only concern being to the animal which he repeatedly declared was 'an alfired good colt.' (Annett I, p. 688).

It is of interest to note that in the census of the town taken in 1873 the following people are listed as residents on our home farm (Lot 21 Range 6): Dexter Pierce, age 45; Mary E., 42; James M., 21; Loren D., 19; Willie B., 17; Jessie G., 13; Austin O., 11; Myron E., 8; and Jane L., 4. Listed on the other farm (Lot 20 Range 6) were: Addison Pierce, age 56; Millie, 60; Clark M., 20; Carrie, 18.

Dexter died on our home farm August 19, 1875, age 48, the same year as the afore mentioned story of Austin. From the inventory of his estate (refer to Appendix pp 10-11)he owned: three cows, two yearlings, two calves, two pigs, twelve turkeys, and sixteen hens. The crops and food items were: hay, corn fodder (animal food), straw, corn, oats, apples, potatoes, butter, pork, and beans. He had several wagons but no carriage. The furnishings were typical of a common farm household. From the tools it can be understood he was farming a self-sufficient farm and doing some woodlot work. They must have had sheep for they listed wool.

Their daughter Jane L. (Jean L. in some sources) was born on this farm and was only six at the time her father died. The family continued to live here until they sold in 1887. Jane had died three years earlier in 1884 in the same month and day she was born, Dec. 7th.; she was 16 years old. The heirs sold the farm, including land and buildings, to Edward H. Dillon and Jennie Dillon for $800.00.

✿

Jennie Dillon and Edward H. Dillon resided here for 15 years. During the time they lived here Mark Twain's *The Adventures of Huckleberry Finn* appeared (1884) and Emily Dickinson's poems were first read (1890). While they resided here four children were born to the Dillons: Fred E., Oscar Joseph, Nellie May, and Harold Edward. When Edward sold the farm he and his family removed to the village of Jaffrey where he operated, with his son Oscar, a garage and livery service business (Annett, p. 244). I was not able to find much written about the Dillons while they were living on the farm, but at one time a woman who shopped at our farm stand told me she was related to the Dillons and she happened to be residing a mile up the back road from here in a summer residence that was in the Dillon family. From the town tax records I was able to understand the size and type of farming he conducted here. It was 125 acres and the Dillons had over the years from one to nine cows, one to three sheep, and one to three hogs. The town records listed him owning first one carriage, from 1890 until 1895, and then two carriages for several years. That was the first they were taxed by the town and appeared on records. Jennie Dillon wrote her name in light blue in our garage with the date of 1887, and it is still there today. Funny, I only recently discovered it, and it has been there so long, but then I just became aware of Jennie through my research. Archie says we should remove the board to save it. Maybe we will someday.

✿

On September 29, 1899, Jennie Dillon sold to Jules Duval 130 acres, land and buildings for $1,300.00. Upon his arrival in Jaffrey in 1886 from Quebec Province, Canada, Jules worked in the local mills. He was then engaged in farming here until 1919. Children of his and Roseanna born on this farm were: Mea Courinne, September 20, 1901, and Renne Avard, born July 10, 1905. They also had two older children who had come with them from Quebec. Mea Courinne was the first one to tell me about living on this farm and aroused the fascination in me as to who was here before us. She was a customer in our earlier farm stand and very casually mentioned to me one day, "I was born in that house." I asked her, "Whereabouts?" She replied, "In the back corner bedroom." That room is now our bathroom, and I always wondered why it was as large as it is. It was the "borning room" back then and was converted to a bathroom sometime in the 1920-30s by the Jurva family. Previous to that they had an outhouse in the back corner of the woodshed, now our living room.

✣

Frank and Hilda Hyrk purchased the farm from Jules Duval on July 14, 1919, and then sold it to Charles and Fannie M. Jurva on October 3, 1921: 130 acres, land and buildings. At first Charles lived in Worcester, Massachusetts and came up by train to the farm where he stayed and worked during the week and returned home on the weekend; this was before purchasing the farm and moving his family here. Four years after the move a daughter, Thelma Helena, was born here May 7, 1925. She joined an older sister, Toini Irene, seven, and a brother, Tauno Charles, six. In my interview with Toini she told the story of coming home from school one day. As she and her brother neared the farmhouse it was quiet, and they did not smell any cookies baking for their after-school snack as they usually did. Their father came to the door and told them they had a baby sister. They were very surprised, because they did not even know a baby was expected! It was very happy news and a pleasant memory.

Charles Jurva operated the farm as a dairy farm, as had some of the preceding owners, and had a retail milk business. He had customers who came to the farm for their milk, and he also made home deliveries. They milked as many as 28 cows, all by hand, both morning and evening.

With the Jurva family, I began to learn about and meet in person a number of people who actually grew up in our home. One person, Norman Peard, worked and lived on the farm for six years and I had an enlightening and enjoyable interview with him. He is a local businessman, former owner/operator of Red's, Inc. (gas station, oil company, disposal service), and I knew he had lived here so I requested an interview with him. He graciously accepted and came to our home one day last fall (1997). He sat at the kitchen table and told me about his life. Norman's father died when he was two years old and at the age of ten he was sent to Thompson School for Boys, located on Thompson Island out in Boston Harbor, a school for boys whose fathers had died. His mother was not able to care for him because she worked as a housekeeper for a family in Jaffrey, and so this was a solution for his care and education. He hated school and Thompson Island and ran away, actually swimming to Boston then hitching rides to Wakefield, Massachusetts. Because he had left, he was not allowed to return and so was sent to his mother. With the help of the selectmen she was able to find a family willing to have 13-year-old Norman live with them and work for his room and board. He went to school for a short period of time, but then one day he called the superintendent and told him he did not want to attend school any longer. His reasoning convinced the superintendent to allow him to quit school. He lived and worked at the Jurva farm until he was 18 years old.

Charles and Fannie spoke mainly Finnish and their English was very difficult for Norman to understand, but he liked living and working on the farm. They treated him like family. He shared a room with their son Tauno, and if Tauno got new shoes, Norman got new shoes. They gave him presents at Christmastime just as they did their own children. Fannie Jurva also remembered the neighbor's children, who were poor. Norman has memories of going out through the woods on a sleigh to their farm with gifts for the family.

All the milking was done by hand, and all the water for the cows and other animals was pumped by hand. It was a tough job; cows consume a lot of water in a day. Norman had every third Sunday off after the milking was done. In the summer the Jurvas did haying for other farmers. They were known for doing a good job cleaning the edges of the fields and thus were hired to return the next season. In the winter they cut ice on Cheshire Pond for their refrigeration needs. They brought it back to the icehouse and packed it in sawdust, which kept the ice through the summer. Charles Jurva did not trust electricity and when it became available he did not want to hook onto it. He chose instead to install gaslights in his home. When we moved here in 1961 there was still a gaslight fixture in the hallway, and when we exposed the beam ceiling in the kitchen, there were the gas pipes. Charles made the gas in a well out back, using carbide which they had to go to Fitchburg, Massachusetts, by train to purchase.

Fannie was a good cook. Norman said they ate well and the home was clean and neat. He remembers when Fannie and daughter Thelma traveled to Finland by ship for the summer. He also remembers Fannie as a fast talker.

Thelma answered a questionnaire for me, although I have also talked with her in person on several occasions. Thelma was the baby girl born to Fannie and Charles in 1925, mentioned earlier in the story. She was a lovely woman who has been gracious and willing to share with me her story and pictures. I am indebted to her for her generosity, for it is when people tell me these interesting remembered details that my research comes alive. She sent me some wonderful old pictures of the farm and her parents and one of her helping her father to plow with the horse. She died recently in Holden, Massachusetts. The following is her written response to my questions concerning life on the farm from her perspective. I include the whole piece because it brings her daily life alive and also provides a wonderful picture of farm life in the 1920s and 1930s.

> "Growing up on the farm was like being in the Garden of Eden. We had a pine grove (hurricane of 1938 did damage, however, but remained a favorite area), blueberry bushes—high and low, a brook to swim in, good food, woods, wildflowers, etc. Being the youngest, I was spared

chores and allowed to study and play. In some ways I wish I had learned to work harder. However, I could observe my mother preparing food and baking bread and doing a lot to make our home pleasant. My father got up a 4:00 AM. He made coffee for my mother. She got up later. He went off on his milk route delivery to townspeople. In those days we were proud to have the highest fat content in milk—therefore cream rose to the top of the bottles—before pasteurization began. My mother also worked hard, cooking and canning, doing laundry; she enjoyed her home. She loved to entertain her friends and prepared delicious meals for visitors and for my Clark University Bicycle Club in 1943, when we came to the farm enroute to Mt. Monadnock.

"My parents discussed business together. My mother was a feminist without being aware of it. She was equal. My father treated her that way. They would discuss buying dairy cattle, etc. My parents hoped that my brother would continue the family business, but he was rather shy perhaps, not as outgoing as my father and preferred to do things mechanical. Then he went into the Army after leaving Jaffrey.

"We were happy and felt as we did not lack material goods. My mother and I were able to go to Finland for four months in 1938. That was big news then and our picture was on the front page of the *Jaffrey Recorder and Monadnock Breeze* along with my write-up of the trip. I was born in 1925 so there was the depression to be lived through which we did not feel because we were able to hire help. People even worked to payoff their milk bills. Then World War II came along and farming was difficult without help.

"In school we had good teachers who were very dedicated and to whom we owe many thanks. It was a nice town to live in. The druggist, Mr. Duncan, knew every child's name. The policemen were highly respected.

"We had Christmas Eve celebrations with neighbors-the Lehtinen family [author of the town histories]. We exchanged gifts on Christmas Eve. My mother celebrated the Summer Solstice-June 21st.-which is St. John's Day in Scandinavia and also called Juhannus in Finnish. We had company from the city as well as from nearby towns. My parents had lived in Worcester, Massachusetts, where Toini and Tauno were born. I was born on the farm. We traveled to Michigan several times (and Europe as I mentioned) and to the World's Fair in New York City.

"We ate well and had many, many good meals of beef and veal and vegetables—summer salad of potatoes with cut-up beets, carrots, and herring. Picking blueberries was a favorite activity for my mother particularly. She could meditate in the blueberry fields and really loved picking berries and then making desserts.

"I was alone more because I was younger so I read, wrote plays, and looked forward to visits from the Coll girls and Beverly Deschenes and Eunice Deschenes, from town. The bus took us to school. Mr. Sirois [Archie's grandfather] was our driver. He was very nice. My brother and sister drove early, I learned to drive much later, after leaving Jaffrey. We went to church in Fitchburg to the Lutheran Church sometimes, as there was no Finnish church in town. Toini and I went to the Congregational Church in Jaffrey. I still have the Bible given to me by Reverend Gerald Parker in 1935. My mother knew the Bible by heart in Finnish and often entertained ministers of various denominations."

Toini, the oldest Jurva child, came to Jaffrey from Florida in September 1997 for a visit, as she does about every other year, and gave me an interview. One summer, Thelma and Toini came together and enjoyed reminiscing with friends and visiting places they remembered from childhood. It was so good they did that, for now Thelma is gone. Toini has come to visit us many times over the years we have lived here, sometimes alone and sometimes with family or friends. Each time she likes to see the house and the changes we have made. She takes pride in the changes and in the farm store and farm as a whole. I love having her come for visits, and it gives me a chance to learn more about the farm and the people who lived here.

We found an old, intact, glass milk bottle with Charles Jurva's name printed on it in orange lettering somewhere on the farm. We had it on display in the farm stand when a granddaughter (Norma Jurva) was visiting from Florida. I used to baby-sit Norma and her older sister Nancy. Norma asked, "Would you sell me my grandfather's old milk bottle? I would love to have it to remind me of my grandfather and the farm." I replied, "It is the only one we have, but if I find another I would gladly give you one." A short time later someone in town found one in his basement and sold it to us. Now we had two and Charles had two granddaughters! I ended up giving one bottle to Norma and one to Nancy, for they were Charles's grandchildren, and I thought they each should have one. Well, Archie was sort of upset with me for giving the bottles away. This was a few years ago and we have not been able to find another milk bottle to replace them. We will keep trying, of course, but a part of me regrets giving away both of them, and yet I know that Norma and Nancy will cherish them.

Toini then spoke about her mother. Her parents came to the United States from Finland in August 1913 and resided in Worcester, where she and Tauno were born before the family moved to Jaffrey in 1921. Charles was one of 12 children but the only one to come to this country. Fanny was an educated woman

Cultivating Life
A Story of Earth and Hearth

who loved books. Toini told me she did not go into the barn; in fact, "she would not touch the tit of a cow." But when I was talking with Norman Peard, he told me Mrs. Jurva could milk a cow faster and better than Mr. Jurva. He said, "I was told that in Finland only women did the milking, not the men." A little controversy but not of significance as far as I am concerned; people each remember things differently. When life on the farm became too much for Fannie, she would pack a suitcase and walk to the bottom of the hill, push up the flag for the train to stop, board the train, and go to Worcester for a few days. I can relate to her very well. At times I, too, need to get away for a few days. She liked to entertain and they kept the parlor for the minister's visits.

They had two hired men besides Norman, who lived here in the house, and Fannie had to feed and house them. Toini has memories of delivering milk with her father early in the morning before attending school. The year she graduated from high school, she and her mother drove their Durant car out to Michigan where they visited Finnish friends.

Toini wrote a book about her life on this farm. She titled the book, "The Milkman's Daughter." I am so thankful to Thelma, Toini, and Norman Peard for sharing with me their memories of life on this farm. They were the only living people available to me to learn from. In the 33 years they lived here much was happening in the world. I often wonder how the Jurva family was affected by these events. Aviation was making the news with Charles A. Lindbergh's flight in the *Spirit of St. Louis* across the Atlantic from New York to Paris on May 21, 1927, and Amelia Earhart became the first woman to fly the Atlantic on June 17, 1928. Thelma mentioned the World's Fair, so I know that was of importance to them; it lasted for two years, 1939-1940. The Agricultural Marketing Act was passed to give stability to farm prices in 1928 and then the stock market crashed on Oct. 29, 1929. The impact, according to Thelma, was greater during WW II, because they were not able to acquire hired help. After the crash and during the Depression they still had food to eat and people would work for them to pay off their milk bills.

Toini is going strong at age 82—she is very healthy and swims and exercises daily. Charles and Fannie moved to Vermont to live with Toini when they sold the farm to my grandfather in 1954. They lived to be a good age and enjoyed their family and friends to the very end.

✡

Even though I have only met a few face-to-face, I now have the pleasure of "knowing" the many people who called this their "place." I was moved and exhilarated when I saw their signatures, read their compassionate wills and deeds and realized they actually lived and worked here day in and day out. Some were born here and some died here. I came to know them as intimately as possible, especially because they lived in the very same house and worked on the very same land I now live and work on. They, too, experienced plowing, planting, harvesting. They also viewed the gorgeous sunrises and spectacular sunsets, the same as Archie and I do today. Their children had animals to love and care for, and they ran and played over the same fields and woods, enjoying the same activities our children did and grandchildren do. They lived in this old farmhouse, and I feel strongly that it is because of their history that we today enjoy life here as they did, between the same walls, under the same roof, with good family values and a lifestyle we so enjoy.

The hours and hours spent researching have flown by. Digging for the facts and figures that would help me to know these people and their lives better has been exciting and has given meaning to my overall understanding of them. Since we have lived here, property values and taxes have increased from $84.02 (land, buildings, and livestock) in 1956 to $11,453.36 (land and buildings) in 1997. We have removed buildings (barn, icehouse, slaughterhouse, machinery shed) and built many new ones (two farm stands, egg production plant, two poultry buildings, three greenhouses). The house is constantly evolving. At present there is talk of a new farm store. The production of the farm has increased over time; first it achieved subsistence with a bit of a cash crop; then came 28 cows and a milk business; then a whole diversified industry! Our farm is representative of the history of New England agriculture and its relation to the European settlement of North America: the changes with railroads, with tractors, the shift in production, the markets, the need for money as production required more and more things manufactured elsewhere. Change is the only sure thing! I know there are hundreds of secrets still not known and probably they never will be, but I have gained a sense of what life was like here on the farm before we came, and we have the pleasure of living, working, and raising our family on the same soil, under the same roof, for as long as we stay here.

"Every generation enjoys the use of a vast hoard bequeathed to it by antiquity, and transmits that hoard, augmented by fresh acquisitions to future ages."

Thomas Macaulay

Cultivating Life
A Story of Earth and Hearth

**Jules Duval photos
1899-1919**

Thelma and Charles Jurva 1936

Fannie and Charles Jurva 1950

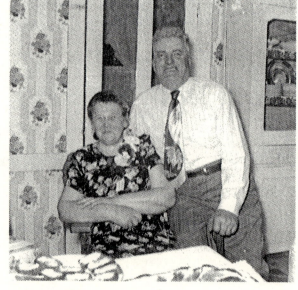

CHAPTER TWO

FARMING: Beginning a new way of life

"They were raised on farms and learned much of what they know from their ancestors. They get genuine satisfaction out of seeing hay in the loft, silage in the silo, canned food lining the cellar walls, and newly plowed fields. Their lives are dictated by weather patterns, seasons, the needs of their livestock, and the demands of their land. Most they love what they do and are determined to continue."
                    Joan Anderson, *The American Family Farm.*

NEW JERSEY TO NEW HAMPSHIRE: The Move of a Lifetime

November 1, 1951, was a cold, gray, windy day. Our 1949 wood-sided Plymouth beach wagon pulled into the driveway of our "new home." My father, mother, and two brothers and I were now going to live on a dairy farm high on a hill with a gorgeous view of another farm, a valley with a river running through it, and a long, continuous, mountain range stretching across the horizon. The wind on the hill was so strong I thought I might be blown away. I remember getting out of the car and then getting right back in. It was so cold. I felt very lost, lonely, and completely unsure of my future. In New Jersey my father worked for his father in a nursery and landscape business along with his older brother. He had attended a technical high school and had taken agricultural courses at Rutgers University. He also grew potatoes and sweet corn to sell in the fresh market in Newark. His dream was owning a dairy farm. He read many agricultural periodicals, in fact that is where an advertisement for the farm appeared, and he and my mother diligently saved their money to purchase this dream farm with a gorgeous view. He was 39 years old when we moved to New Hampshire and began dairy farming.

We moved when I was 20 days short of being 13 years old and in the 8th grade. I had always lived in the same two-story, six-room house in Wyckoff, New Jersey. It was a suburban community with houses and yards side by side and back to back. I left behind every relative and friend I knew. On the block where I lived there were three girls in my grade, Brenda, Arlene, and Alma, and we had grown up together. Just the evening before, the girl across the street, Arlene, and I sat out front on the low stone wall and cried because I was leaving. I could have stayed for the remainder of the school year and lived with my grandparents and thus graduated with my class from 8th grade, but I was up for the adventure my family was embarking on and did not want to be left behind. I remember one of my schoolteachers, Mrs. Mickens, trying to convince me to stay for the year so as to not interrupt my course of studies. I loved and respected Mrs. Mickens, but I could not stay. My school friends gave me a surprise Halloween costume "going away" party. It was a fun night, but I was also sad and felt in some way I was already missing from the picture.

My paternal grandparents lived next door to us, and my brothers and I were their only grandchildren. Just as my friends cried, so did my grandfather, only I didn't find this out until years later when my grandmother told me. It was difficult to think of my grandfather crying. Only now that I am a grandparent can I fully understand how they felt. You see, six of our grandchildren live on various lots on our farms and two others are only a half hour away. They are all very close to us in every way. I would miss them terribly if they were to move several hours away.

When we walked into the house, there in the kitchen was a long, gray, backless, bench. We all put our things on it and then began taking everything off of it, for it was the only place to sit. When we looked around the house, I thought it looked old and decrepit. There were 13 rooms on two floors and a large attic. The kitchen didn't even have a stove. The only good thing was that I would have my own bedroom. All through my early years I always shared a room—first with my older brother Bob and then with younger brother Ed. Now I would have a very large, 14-foot-square bedroom with a mantelpiece in it, three windows and three doors. The ceiling was painted pink, not a pretty pink but a yellowish, peachy kind of pink with many cracks in it. I remember many nights lying there looking up at that ceiling with thoughts of every kind. A drawback of the room was that my parents had to walk through it to get to the bathroom. Complete privacy was something I never had at home.

The first order of business was for my mother to go to a neighboring town and buy an electric stove for cooking and a small wood-burning stove to heat the kitchen. The remainder of the house would be heated by a kerosene parlor stove in the living room and an a electric heater to plug in to warm the bathroom. Needless to say, it was a very cold house. Every morning and evening the kerosene would have to be carried up from the barrel in the cellar and poured into the stove. In the morning my bedroom was so cold I would get up and run to the bathroom, plug in the small electric heater, and put my clothes on it to warm them before dressing up. I never slept in a heated bedroom until I was married (and then I really didn't need it!)

The moving van with our furniture and possessions was late in arriving. We had driven the 245 miles on winding Route 202 from Wyckoff, New Jersey, to

*Cultivating Life
A Story of Earth and Hearth*

Jaffrey, New Hampshire, in eight hours, having left very early in the morning. The moving van had to make the same trip but it took a lot longer.

Friends of my mother's, Gus and Al Gerken, who had also moved from New Jersey to New Hampshire a couple of years before, came down from their home in Bradford, an hour away, to greet us. They brought a huge pot of spaghetti sauce for our dinner. Finally someone shouted, "Here comes the moving van!" It was very long and low and proceeding slowly up the hill and into the driveway. It was already afternoon. The men set about quickly unloading our furniture and possessions. A problem arose when they discovered neither the front or the back stairways could take the bedroom furniture. The front stairway had two corners in it, and the back stairway was completely enclosed and had a door at the top and one at the bottom (to conserve heat). So they had to remove a window, casing and all, hand up all the large pieces of furniture over the porch and pass them through the enlarged opening. They worked quickly and nonstop until the huge house had furniture in it and looked somewhat like "home."

The new electric range arrived by suppertime and the women set about heating the sauce and cooking the spaghetti. We ate our first meal in our "new home" in the large red and white kitchen sort of picnic style—paper goods not dishes. Our welcoming family left after supper and we were then alone, completely alone in the farmhouse. But out in the barns were the milking cows, calves, pigs, and chickens that needed attention. I do not remember much about the animals and barns right off. I think I was mainly concerned with settling in my new room and experiencing my surroundings.

The very next day we were to go to school. I woke up in bad pain from the dysmenorrhea I suffered from all my adolescent years and could not go to school. My mother took my brothers down and registered them, Bob, a junior in high school, and Ed, a second grader, and they went for the day. I then had to go alone the next day. I was very scared but tried hard not to show it. I remember the kids telling me I talked funny and they would ask me to say different words, but I thought <u>they</u> sounded funny and I could not understand some of their words, especially those with R's in them. The town had a large population of French-Canadian descendants and I could not pronounce their names. Ones I had particular difficulty with were: Courchene, Letourneau, LaFreniere, Rabidoux, Sirois, Cournoyer, Archambault. I would say "car" and they would say "ka". They would laugh when I said "water" or "garage." I now realize that part of me felt special, different, like a celebrity (sort of), and part of me wanted to be just like everyone else. I did enjoy being "the new girl" for a time.

Life became full of contrasts for me, which was very new and different from anything I had experienced before. Two ways I was different and special from the other girls were: I could sew very well and made my own clothes, and I had been a Girl Scout for many years growing up in New Jersey. I feel the scouting experience helped to build my self-esteem and sense of security all through my high school years. I was a fairly popular girl and did not lack friends or attention.

Through the years, from time to time, I have given some thought as to what life would have been like if I had not moved. In New Jersey I would have been just another girl,—not different, not special, not worthy of attention out of the ordinary. I would probably have continued to be just an average student. Life would have just moved along without special happenings or meanings. Wyckoff and Jaffrey had the same population in 1951, but Jaffrey had more stores and industry. Due to strict zoning, Wyckoff prohibited industry, and apartment houses, allowing only residences. It is a "bedroom town" of New York City, but in a rural setting. People's values are different from those in Jaffrey. Appearances, physical and material, matter too much in New Jersey, and the pace of life is much faster. In New Hampshire we look inward more and are more accepting of different nationalities and economic backgrounds.

My final feelings on our "big move" have always been the same: I am glad we moved to New Hampshire to live on a farm in small-town New England. I met my husband and we have raised our children here and have continued to live here, in the same neighborhood, since 1951. No regrets, only joys!

Cultivating Life
A Story of Earth and Hearth

Our Wedding Day—May 3, 1958

CHAPTER THREE

KNEE HIGH BY THE FOURTH OF JULY
An old saying pertaining to the readiness of sweet corn.

"...whoever could make two ears of corn, or two blades of grass, to grow upon a spot of ground where only one grew before, would deserve better of mankind, and do more essential service to his country, than the whole of race of politicians put together."
Swift, *Gulliver: Voyage to Brobdingnag*.

It was a hot and sultry August day in 1965, one that made you sweat without actually doing anything, when my father came over to have a conversation with me about the surplus sweet corn he had. My three young children were interrupting us and running around. They were calling to their grandfather, "Swing me like an aeroplane, Grandpa, swing me." Another one yelled, "Me first, me first" and another "Swing ME, swing ME." After swinging each of the kids Daddy wiped his face with his large handkerchief and began to tell me about planting some sweet corn for old Mr. Kennedy, down on the Rindge Road, because the new Route 202 road had taken his corn fields and farm stand. Daddy had a corn planter to plant the cow corn he grew to cut for ensilage to feed the cows in winter, and so he offered to plant some sweet corn. Well, old Mr. Kennedy could not begin to pick all the corn and he couldn't sell that much either, so Daddy was offering it to me to sell.

At this time my husband, Archie, was still working for his father full time on his farm plus managing our own farm. That evening I told Archie about the corn, and he agreed to pick some the next day. He found an old wooden board, at least 12 inches wide and about seven feet long, with a natural point broken on one end, forming a good arrow. That night I painted the board white on both sides and lettered it in bright red letters, SWEET CORN. The point he placed so people passing on the highway (Route. 202) would know to turn and drive up the hill to get the corn. We then placed two saw horses and several large planks of wood across them to form a table out in the front yard of our house between the very large, old sugar Maple trees. That was the beginning of our farm stand, and to this day sweet corn is our major crop and best "drawing" for customers.

The sign on the highway worked well; people drove up the hill to buy fresh-picked corn. The kids thought it great fun to sell something to people. Our first cash drawer was an old, round, wooden box with a cover on it originally made here in Jaffrey. We continued to use it for a number of years before finally going to a cash register. In the beginning all figuring was done on the paper bags we bagged the produce in. The first year was a short season, but the next year Archie planted the corn in smaller lots, spacing the plantings so we would have fresh corn for a longer season. He now starts planting around April 20th and plants every five days until July 8-10. The second year we again used the table under the trees in front of our home with the circular driveway to sell from. The kids would often get to the customers first and start the transaction before I came out of the house. Early in their lives they learned about "making money." The first year we sold corn Suzanne was six, Mark was four, and Peggy was three. Our youngest, David, arrived three years later. Suzanne liked selling the corn and bagging it up, and Mark liked to help pick it. He was very strong and always my "right-hand man" when Archie was away working all day. I remember very clearly one day in particular that he came to my rescue. When we first moved to our farm there were many snakes that we encountered almost daily the first few summers. With no one living here for awhile they thought they had the place to themselves. They kept surprising me and I do not like snakes. One day I encountered a large one when in the barnyard with the children and I screamed. Mark said, "Wait, I'll get it!" He climbed fast over the barway gate, ran to get a hoe, came back, tossed the hoe over the gate, and proceeded to climb back over it even faster, and killed the snake! I was so impressed and very thankful. What a brave four-year-old.

    The second year we sold corn, people would ask for tomatoes, summer squash, cucumbers and the like. We would go to our own garden to pick what we had and sell it. The farm stand idea was blossoming! After that year, in the wintertime, Archie and I talked about purchasing a small, three-sided building for our "new" farm stand. Very often our dinnertime ended with the family discussing business matters. "What do you think about buying Mr. Grummon's old stand building and moving it here?" Archie asked. As the profits increased we felt we needed a more permanent place to sell from in all kinds of weather. It was an exciting day when the long, low, flat trailer truck pulled up with the building on the bed. The kids and I ran to see this happening. They rolled it off on pipes and put it on the field across the road from our home. Archie then built shelves inside the three walls and made a table for the middle area. Mark was right there helping out and observing everything his father did. He has a natural talent for working with his hands on wood and machinery. Suzanne and Peggy would help with the picking and selling, although we did not expect them to work. They all had a lot of free time and enjoyed playing Matchboxes together by the hour. They would build a town or farm with twig trees and moss fields and make little buildings from boxes. We got so busy I could not just run out of the house to a table to sell; I had to stay at the stand and sell. That soon became

Helen Coll

a problem for I was unable to get other work done for "minding the stand" all day. And so we hired a young school girl, Ann, to help during some hours of each day. She was our first employee of many, many to come.

Some of the early customers stayed with us for years, many until they died, and I began to feel the losses as if they were family. Because I saw them almost daily and had conversations of personal detail, I became very close to them. I remember Mr. Buckwold, a dear man, shy but always with a few words to share with me about gardening, or his wife; Mr. Burgoyne, also quiet but a pleasure to see drive up; and Mr. & Mrs. Silver, who always disagreed about what or how much to purchase. I was once quoted in an interview saying, "Archie likes a satisfied customer." That is very true! He is motivated by that more than any other single thing. He has a capacity for being happy, friendly, and very willing to please, and our customers over the years have responded to those qualities and to our fresh foods.

With our first farm stand, people pulled up to it and got out to buy. I knew them by their cars and license plates and by their pets. That was something I missed when we built the next larger stand (in 1976) that is now enclosed. I no longer had that connection and I also didn't see their dogs any more. Changes and more changes, some good, some not so good. We now are at the point of another expansion. We have been talking about it for a year or so. We are too crowded and need more display and checkout area. Also, we now have become a farm store, rather than a farm stand, for we carry a full line of grocery items as well as our fresh eggs and produce. In the beginning of the farm stand we often talked about whether we should stay at our farm location or move onto the highway. We have consciously chosen to stay on the farm site and promote farm life in the beautiful setting we have on this hilltop with gorgeous pastoral views. Being on the highway would have been more appealing to the transient customer, not local people. We have now built our business and reputation to the point of a very high customer flow and even have busloads of people come to enjoy the farm, the view, and the products.

All through the years that we have operated the farm stand, we have also raised laying hens and produce, packed and marketed eggs every day of the year from our 50,000 hens. Early in our farm operation we were able to save the vegetable money to help pay the grain bill when winter came. We learned a very valuable lesson for success in farming—diversification. Another valuable tool is direct marketing. This requires a lot of time and commitment but is essential to the survival of agriculture on the family farm. The farm stand and the egg production complement each other and ease the burden of relying solely on one form of agriculture, whose markets and seasons can affect the overall picture of profit and loss. Sweet corn requires a lot of nitrogen, and chicken manure is the highest in nitrogen of any natural fertilizer; so again, one helps the other.

Cultivating Life
A Story of Earth and Hearth

Archie's dad was in the broiler industry, but that business began to move to the southern states and he was operating at a loss. He chose not to change or diversify because he was getting older and decided to retire from farming. The saying "Don't put all your eggs in one basket" is so true for us, as it is for many farmers. Do not solely depend on one basket (one product or crop) to carry all that is important to you. On a small family farm this is even more difficult, for you are multiplying the areas of responsibility and the aspects of the business you need to be in close and accurate contact with to assure a profit.

In our operation nothing is accidental. Archie and I discuss everything and at great length and over a period of time before we make any decisions or changes or purchases. We began the growing of sweet corn by chance, but from there on all was carefully orchestrated for optimum success. Would we change anything? I feel confident (Archie agrees) we have done what we needed to do each step along the path, which has led us through 32 years of a successful and rewarding farm stand operation.

Sweet corn, as I stated earlier, is our main crop. Archie has been quoted, "We kind of built our reputation on corn." There are many varieties of sweet corn: some are all yellow, some yellow and white and some all white. The first corn we grew was Agway's Butter and Sugar, a two-color, very sweet, tender corn that was difficult to get even growth on, which made it hard to pick and have consistent ripeness. Some all-yellow varieties are the old-time, small ear Golden Bantam (my father grew this in New Jersey for wholesale marketing), Country Gentlemen, also an old variety with very large ears, and Seneca Gold, which we grew for awhile. An all-white variety that has been around for a long time and we still grow is Silver Queen. It produces large, sweet ears and is a favorite of many people, but it takes a full 95 days to mature. Sweet corn can vary from 60 to 95 days to maturity, depending on variety.

The propagation of butter and sugar varieties changed the sweet corn market forever. People call it by various names: butter and cream, salt and pepper, or sugar and gold, but it is all butter and sugar. The different varieties also produce different size ears: large ears, fat ears, skinny ears, long ears, and short ears. Some people like it full (meaning more color and larger kernels), and some like it young (very light in color and small, round kernels). There are many opinions as to what is "good" corn. The taste of corn can be compared to a good wine; there are many different stages of growth (maturity) and varieties. There is the milk stage, when corn is tender and juicy. Then the mealy stage, when it is drier and requires more chewing. When it is mushy, it is no longer marketable. Some people like the feel of small kernels in the mouth and some prefer larger, fuller texture. There are varieties that are very sweet or ones that have strong corn flavor or ones with very little flavor but are tender. We try our best to satisfy everyone (not quite possible), but we know when corn is at its peak, and we try to pick it then and sell it as soon as possible. Mr. Pike always wants his corn very young; he likes tiny kernels. You can tell a lot about the ripeness of the corn inside the husk by feeling through the husk; feel for fullness and firmness. We try to discourage people from opening or stripping the ears. It lasts much better and stays fresher if the ears remain unopened. One customer, Mrs. Moore, actually gets mad at people for opening the ears. She will tell them straight out not to open and spoil them for others. You see, some people open the ear and then put it back on the shelf and take another one, unopened. At one time we had a young girl, Bithy, working for us who liked to draw, and she drew a picture of an embarrassed ear of corn saying, "Please don't strip the corn." The sign, as well as Mrs. Moore, are ignored by some customers.

We used to grow "standard" sweet corn or normal sweet corn which had rich corn flavor, but the quality was best when picked and cooked quickly or at least the same day. We now grow sugar enhanced corn which is a variety of sweet corn that retains its sweetness several days after it is picked, because moisture loss is slower than in normal sweet corn and tenderness is improved, resulting in a sweeter, more tender kernel with good corn flavor that will retain good quality longer. At this time Lancelot is our favorite. For several years we grew a butter and sugar corn called Burgundy. It was a small ear, had burgundy color on the husk, and was very sweet and tender. We had to stop growing it because we could no longer buy the seed. My all-time favorite was called Deep Gold. It was not deep gold at all; in fact it was fairly light yellow and had small kernels on a larger ear. I loved it, but we could not buy the seed for that variety either. Every day of the growing season (end of July to the beginning of October) we eat corn. At supper the conversation goes like this: "Try this ear!" "What variety is this ear?" "Boy, this is sweet and tender!" Remember 'such & such' kind?" Why are the seed companies always changing varieties?" "Now this is perfect!" Archie is always sampling the corn while picking it. He taste tests it raw in the field, and he also cooks it in the microwave at the stand. We truly enjoy this product/crop of our efforts and our many customers do also!

The leaves on the cornstalk are rough and can cause minor skin abrasions that make some people itch. One of our grandsons worked picking corn this summer, and he is allergic to the corn husks. He has to wear a long-sleeved shirt to pick in so he will not be covered with an itchy rash. The height of the stalk varies with varieties, but generally it is five-six feet tall. Each one has two to three ears on it, mostly two, but usually only one is sellable. When it is ready, the cornsilk, which comes out of the top of the ear, will turn brown. Each thread of cornsilk is attached to each kernel of corn on the cob. It is necessary for Archie to check the corn every day to see the stage of ripeness. Entire fields can mature and go by if not picked at the peak of ripeness. Recently Archie and I were in Mexico to attend the wedding of an exchange student, Ileana, whom we had hosted a few years ago. At her reception we were served a first-course soup. It was cream and brown in color and tasted something like mushroom. When I inquired of Ileana's mother, "What kind is it?" she told me, "It is cream corn soup made from the fungus that grows on corn." Well, we call that corn smut and we throw it away! Corn is so important in the Mexican diet that they use every part they can.

I particularly like driving the tractor to pick the corn, for from the seat I can look out over a waving sea of golden tassels to the edges of the fields. Some fields are surrounded by tall pine trees, which create interesting light and shadow pictures and which in some years are loaded with pine cones at the very top. It is said the more pine cones, the colder and snower the winter, and this year that proved true. Other fields are on the crest of hills and the view above the tassels is gorgeous scenery of mountains and endless sky. On the ground I often can see animal tracks such as deer and raccoon and bear. The other day a flock of black birds landed on the tassels and then took flight again with a flurry of black wings. In the fall, I see large flocks of Canada geese eating left-behind corn in the fields on their stopover before flying on to the south. Wild turkeys are increasing in number every year. Yesterday I saw a flock of thirty eating in the field across from my house.

We do not own enough acres to grow the quantity of corn we need and so we rent or lease land from other people. One of these pieces of land is located in the town of Sharon. It is a nice, large, open field, great for growing sweet corn. This particular year the field had been planted and the corn was in tassel and needed to be sprayed for corn ear worm. Archie had a very tall, funny looking tractor-sprayer (a Hahn high-boy) which he drove over the tops of the tall corn. He had to sit high up above the corn himself. Well this day he got stuck (the year must have been a wet one) and when the children and I arrived with his lunch, we found him in this dilemma. He had another tractor there for cultivation he was doing and he asked that I drive it and pull his sprayer out from whence it was stuck. I got on the tractor and was driving it so as to pull the sprayer, when I heard the kids yell. I looked back just in time to see Archie flying through the air and the sprayer tipping over in the field. Thankfully he landed on his feet and was not hurt. We sure had a good laugh about Archie's ability to fly and my poor driving and not looking back at what I was pulling. It would have made a good picture or video, but it is now only captured in our minds.

For many years we picked corn in bushel baskets, but now we pick into large 20-bushel bins. We have always picked by hand except for one year, when we tried an automatic corn picker. It did not work for our purposes for there was too much sorting to be done. A cousin of Archie's, who was a machinist by trade, made us a set of fork lifts to put onto the front bucket loader of our tractor to hold the large bins in trade for the apple pumice (what is left after we squeeze the apples for cider) for feeding to his cows. This year our son Mark (now 37) made a fork lift for the back of the tractor. It works very well and can be lifted higher to load the bins onto the truck to drive out of the fields. The only difference is that the tractor must be driven backwards, but for the pickers it is much easier.

After we have picked the fields, the stalks and corn that are left behind people will gather to feed to their cows and pigs. For many summers a local camp came and gleaned the fields for sweet corn to feed campers. We like to make use of everything we can and give others the opportunity to utilize what may go to waste. A couple of years we had a church group come and glean the tomato fields to do canning. It is good to not waste food and to be of help to others in need. Frugality is a fine trait to possess.

In 1988 Archie was featured in a magazine, *New Hampshire Profiles*, as "Our Kind of Hero." A quote from the article written by David J. Gibson about farming was, "It takes a lot of courage, I'll tell you that," says Coll. "You put your money and time and efforts on the line not knowing what the return is going to be...Of course, there were 'iffy' times in the beginning when I wondered if I really would be able to do this to support a family. But things evolved, the demand was there, and you gain more confidence. You've got to love doing it." Archie does love farming and at 63 is still going very strong.

"Work is love made visible."

"And in keeping yourself with labour you are in truth loving life,
And to love life through labour is to be intimate with life's inmost secret."

"And all work is empty save when there is love;
And when you work with love you bind yourself to yourself,
and to one another, and to God."

Kahlil Gibran, *The Prophet*

*Cultivating Life
A Story of Earth and Hearth*

**Left: Old Farm Stand—
1969**

Below: New Farm Stand—2001

Helen Coll

View of all three farms—1998

Cultivating Life
A Story of Earth and Hearth

CHAPTER FOUR

IN THE GARDEN

"I come to the garden alone, while the dew is still on the roses,
And the voice I hear, falling on my ear, the Son of God discloses."
C. Austin Miles, 1912

Early every morning of the growing season, before the dew leaves and the bugs arrive, I am off to the flower garden equipped with my favorite cutting shears and buckets of clean, cool water all in my handy, large, flat garden cart, where I pick flowers for mixed bouquets to sell to our various customers in our farm stand. The hymn "In the Garden" is my theme song as I pick in the cool, quiet morning; I sing it often, as it is so appropriate to my entire life.

In Wyckoff, we lived in the former home of my paternal great-grandparents. They were of Dutch descent and very stern, serious, and religious. They did not celebrate holidays. The first Christmas tree my grandfather Van Blarcom had was after he married my grandmother. As a result of this, he loved to celebrate birthdays, anniversaries, and Christmas. My great-grandmother, Sarah Westervelt Van Blarcom, died the year I turned one, at the age of 85. My paternal grandparents lived next door in a similar two-story house my grandfather built and we shared a driveway. There was a path from our back door to their back door. At times this must have been a difficult arrangement for my mother, and at other times it probably was a blessing. On one hand, she may have felt she was living her life under the constant eye of her husband's parents' scrutiny and approval or disapproval, and on the other hand, they were close by to help out in emergencies with watching children.

Needless to say, we children were very close to our grandparents and they adored us. They did not spoil us at all, but were firm and yet loving. I was fortunate to be raised by industrious, hard-working, conscientious, thoughtful, kind parents and grandparents. They all epitomized middle-class, rural America by their complete self-reliance. They looked only to themselves for everything they needed in life, working very hard to attain their goals and raise their families with care and love and strong discipline, by demonstration and words, not the rod in all areas of life—work, family values, and religion. They believed in resting on the Sabbath: no card playing, sewing, swimming; only being together as family for dinner and a family ride in the car. We had an old, black, Pontiac car with front and back seats and my brothers and I sat in the back, arguing and getting on each others nerves as well as those of my parents. Boring, boring; our Sundays went on forever.

My father worked with his father and brother in a family nursery, landscape, and floral business. It was started by my grandfather's family on his in-law's side (the DeBauns). They had beautiful, old, fieldstone and glass greenhouses for growing cut flowers. To this day the damp fragrance of a greenhouse transports me back to another time and place with such nostalgia for the childhood I enjoyed. I am reminded of my first job. I was given the task of putting the foil paper onto potted plants we were selling for Easter. My "pay" was to choose something from the garden shop I would like. I chose a small pottery watering can, such as would be used for a potted plant or cut flowers. I still have it. The nursery was a marvelous place to visit and see my father and grandfather at work. Inside one of the greenhouses there was an ornamental stone garden complete with a waterfall and pond. In the pond were large, orange and white koi (Japanese goldfish), and growing up one side of the falls and arching over and down the other side, was a gorgeous passion flower (meaning stands for belief) plant. (Each flower has a meaning and I will mention them throughout this chapter). The blossoms were spectacular; they had large petals of alternating pink and white with a ring of deep purple spikes in the center. What a sight to encounter! As a child I probably took it for granted; only now looking back do I fully appreciate what it must have been like. On our farm we recently placed a gazebo for the same reasons the fish pond and falls must have been built—to have an esthetically pleasing place for customers to come and enjoy our business. The gazebo is located on a hill with a wonderful view of farms, fields, and sunsets and is a great spot to rest and reflect. Often there are photographs being taken of the gazebo and the view. In the greenhouses they also grew carnations (fascination, woman's love) and snapdragons (presumption). I love the subtle fragrance of each of them. They were started by sowing seeds in trays and then transplanting them to tables, which had raised edges and were filled with soil. When in perfect bloom, they were cut, wrapped, and sold wholesale to floral businesses. Often a worker would give me ones that were not perfect and I would play with them, pulling them apart or just sitting and smelling their beautiful fragrance. These happy, carefree memories are all a part of me,—mind, body, and soul. They conjure up wonderful thoughts of a comfortable, secure childhood.

When I was very young my grandmother and I would take walks in the woods to find wildflowers and then come home to look up the names of them in a large book of wildflowers she always had in her living room. When she was older and could not go with me, I would still bring home wildflowers for us to look up and name. It gives me a warm feeling now, just remembering those times and our being together, sharing our love of flowers and each other.

My grandfather had marvelous flower gardens all around his home. He tended them each day when he came home from work, before and after his supper. I can still visualize him out there in his yard with a white handkerchief, knotted on each corner, and placed onto his bald head to keep the flies from bothering him. It was also handy for wiping his brow of sweat. His yard was always well manicured and beautiful. He built arbors and trellises for roses and grapes to climb, and a stone and brick patio with a fireplace and small wall all around it with an opening to go into it. It was like being in an outdoor play area, possibly from *Alice in Wonderland.* He also built a shuffleboard court for playing enjoyment and landscaped it beautifully. On one side of the house, the shady side, he had a hosta garden: gorgeous green and white, large, leafy plants which in the springtime had lily of the valley growing around them. Lily of the valley (return of happiness) with their slightly curved, slender stalks and tiny white bells hanging down the curve, so very fragrant and sweet. When I was married I carried a bouquet of lily of the valley, probably because of childhood memories of beauty as well as the sense of security.

There were many kinds of trees: blue spruce (hope in adversity), pink dogwood, cherry (education), magnolia (dignity, love of nature), oaks (hospitality), maples (reserve), ornamental red maples. There were also many varieties of shrubs: holly (forgotten, foresight), rhododendrons (danger), azaleas (temperance), mountain laurel (ambition, glory), flowering almond (hope). He also had a large, productive vegetable garden. My grandmother would call to him from the kitchen window, "Please come in for supper and bring some tomatoes with you." He loved tomatoes and ate them everyday of the growing season always with sugar sprinkled on the warm, fresh slices.

One day Grandpa told me, "Go into the house and ask Grandma for a large rag of sheeting." I did just that and brought it to him, and he proceeded to tear it into strips and together we tied them onto a string he had strung across the garden. This was to keep the birds away. Did it work? I don't remember, but I was so pleased to be of help to him. It wasn't often that I could work with him and feel I was doing anything of importance; that is probably why this memory comes back to me now. I learned to can fruits and vegetables from my grandmother and mother. Sometimes my grandmother would have her sister, Aunt Jennie, come and help, and in return she would go to her home and help her can. After I was married, they both came to New Hampshire and helped me can peaches. What a pleasant time we had talking and working at the same time and having a final product to take pride in. They also quilted and did sewing together, and I have memories of them laughing and talking about so many things—a time I would like to return to in this busy rush, rush world. I spent many happy hours learning to sew and crochet with them, and I do think I learned many of life's lessons without even being aware of them while listening to their conversations.

In our yard, my father had the vegetable garden, and my mother had the flower gardens. She loved cut flowers and we always had them in our home. She lovingly arranged them in various vases and they were in most of the rooms. When I was away from home in nurse's training, she would send me back to school with bouquets of flowers. I cherish those thoughts, for they speak to me of her love for me, something she never actually put into words. Many times it was a small, orange Fiesta Ware cream pitcher filled with orange, yellow, and gold nasturtiums (patriotism). Always when I see, smell, or hear of nasturtiums, I instantly think of my mother and a warm feeling washes over me. I still fill the same pitcher with nasturtiums and warm and loving thoughts of her.

Today I grow all the same cut flowers my mother so enjoyed and for many of the same reasons, I am sure—for their beauty, abundant blooms, bright colors, aesthetic appeal, subtle fragrances, and the artistic enhancement they lend to our lives. The varieties I have grown for pleasure and for sale for 30 some years are: giant zinnias (thoughts of absent friends) for their wonderful size and display value; cut-and-come-again zinnias for their many colors, perfect size and shape, and great abundance; giant snapdragons for their beautiful fragrance and unusual appearance; gorgeous pink and purple, delicate cosmos with their feathery greens; asters (variety) also in shades of pink and purple and many types of blooms, some daisy (single petal) shaped, some mum (multi petals) shaped; giant marigolds for their bright oranges and yellows; bachelor buttons in beautiful blues; and some spiky variety flowers such as leaf salvias and tall ageratums for the accents they lend to bouquets.

The giant zinnias are the main flowers in my bouquets; they have large, bright petaled colors of red, orange, pink, purple, yellow, and white. They last long after picking and bloom throughout the entire growing season. The cosmos are the tallest flowers in my garden, sometimes as tall as I. They lend their delicate lavenders and pinks, burgundies and whites, so nicely to the bouquets; they also have the longest stems. The cut-and-come-agains do just that; cut them and they keep coming; they are wonderful and bloom in many colors and petal counts. Every day I cut all the good blooms I can, and the next day I come back and there are just as many to pick again. It never ceases to amaze me, even after all these years. I think I will not have many the next day to chose from and there they are waiting to be admired and picked for everyone's enjoyment. If we have a rainy, cloudy spell of weather they do slow down, and it is more difficult to get enough nice blossoms. I grow many varieties of the same type of flower (zinnias and snaps, for example), so as to have various petal formations and differing colors and heights.

*Cultivating Life
A Story of Earth and Hearth*

Each and every day of the growing season (June to October) I cut about 24 bouquets and each bouquet has 30-36 stems. Now that is a goodly amount of cutting! Each stem is cut with my favorite cutting scissors, a gift from Archie, and the leaves are stripped off, all except the very top ones, between my thumb and middle fingers. Consequently my fingers are permanently stained for the season. No leaves should ever be in the water in an arrangement if you want it to last the longest possible time. Immediately after cutting I place them into buckets of clean water. This is all done very rapidly, as the day is getting warmer and the time for the stand to open is coming nearer. I then take the buckets of flowers to a place where I can quickly count and arrange them and put them into tall, waxed paper cups, the kind used for milk shakes or frappes. They are then put out in a display to sell to the farm stand's daily customers.

At present I get $4.95 for each bouquet. I can remember charging $2.95 years ago but not any lower than that. I tried to get $5.49 last year, but people would not pay that much. Not that they aren't big, beautiful bouquets and worth every penny, but people just would not part with the extra money for a nonnecessity like flowers. I have been getting $4.95 for several years and all my costs over those years have gone up. Everything costs more—from the seeds, to the greenhouse expenses (containers, soil, heat and electricity), labor costs, property taxes, paper goods, everything. But people will not pay more, so I have to settle for what they will pay. A part of me feels cheated and not valued, but I get over it and continue to sell bouquets which add beauty, color, and cheer to people's lives and give me joy and pleasure in doing the job. On the flip side of that, flowers, I feel, should be given away and in the beginning I grew them for the beauty they added to the stand surroundings, and I would cut them and give them away. A part of me still feels that way, but I realistically need to earn money, as does everyone, and this is a way I can accomplish that. There still are times I give away a bouquet—like to someone who is ill, or a grieving customer, or an older person who admires them and tells me about their grandmother growing them or for a special occasion they might mention in conversation. Giving them away benefits the giver as well as the receiver; it lightens everyone's load and brightens their day. I would say I have been quite successful in my flower business; I have a great deal of satisfaction doing the job and people have a lot of joy looking at the garden, buying the flowers, keeping them or giving them away.

My gardens are cutting gardens and so they are not as beautiful as ones created primarily for viewing enjoyment. One of my gardens is located directly next to the farm stand, at the end of the parking lot, and so is very visible to all the customers. People enjoy talking with me and asking questions when I am there picking or weeding and they also like to walk through them and have a closer look for themselves. It is a delight to give joy in this way to people, and that is a lot of the compensation of the job. People frequently tell me how lucky I am to have such a pleasurable job in such a beautiful location. Yes, it is pleasure, but it is also hard work. It always amazes me how little some people know about growing, planting, and picking, but I am here to help educate them as well as sell to them. Some of the questions always surprise me: Do you have to weed them? Water them? Do you plant them every year? How do you decide what to plant? Pick? What about the bees? Insects?

One day many years ago I had a stand customer dig up a large clump of marigolds and bring it to me in the stand on a brown paper bag. She asked me, "How much is this?" I was so shocked I could hardy speak. I asked her, "Where did you get this from?" and she told me, "Out front." I hurried out to look and sure enough she had dug the clump up from the border of beautiful orange and gold marigolds that went along the front of my garden, Now there was this big hole! Imagine the nerve—to dig it up and then ask me to sell it to her. She said, "I have a hole in my garden where a plant died," and so she needed another to replace it and she dug up mine and left a hole! Truly, I was so shocked I ended up giving it to her. I just said, "Take it," and she did. Such a nerve!!

Another time I had a person want, no demand, to cut her own flowers for a wedding she was doing. Because of past problems with people cutting for themselves, I do not let people cut—I do all the cutting. Well, she was convincing and I was busy with customers and so she cut the flowers. When she brought them in to me, she had literally cut the entire plants! She said the vases were very large so she needed them that tall. I had told her 15 cents a stem before she cut them and that was what she said she should pay, but in actuality she was paying 15 cents for a plant! People can be very funny and very exasperating!

Requests over the years have also been odd. Like the woman who wanted a bouquet of only blue bachelor buttons. They were for an elderly lady's 80th birthday party and they were her favorite flower. The lady was Grandmother Yoss who ran the Dublin Inn in Dublin, New Hampshire, and Grandmother's House in Francestown, New Hampshire. She wanted a large bouquet and naturally they were very difficult to pick, as they were small blossoms with very thin stems, and it took many, many stems to make the large bouquet. Then she didn't want to pay what they were worth. Oh well, Grandmother Yoss would be happy!

In the front of the stand greenhouse I have a perennial flower garden. One year a man dug up, mind you without asking, some beautiful yellow lilies (falsehood) I had growing there because he didn't have any in his perennial garden and couldn't find any already blooming. He then brought me some hollyhocks (fecundity) from his garden to replace them. All this a stand employee told me, not the man. I didn't have any hollyhocks, I didn't want any, and furthermore I dislike them! He seemed to think that if you grow them at your place of business, you should be willing to sell them or, as in this case, exchange them!

We had a very dear friend, Erna, who summered for many years at the farm beyond my parents. My father did the haying there and we developed a beautiful friendship over time. They had escaped from the Nazi occupation of Vienna, Austria. Erna's husband, Richard, was the editor of a newspaper in Vienna, and the day the Nazis marched into Vienna they went directly to Richard's office and gave him 24 hours to leave Austria, and he could only take personal possessions with him, no money. He and Erna came to the United States and made their home in Brookline, Massachusetts, until his death. After he died Erna came to the farm to rest, and one day she was at the stand when Archie was there. He extended our deepest sympathy and gave her a bouquet of marigolds. I was sad when he told me he had given her the marigolds, for I knew they were not that fancy or that fresh. When I saw Erna the next week she told me how beautiful the marigolds still were, and how touched she was by Archie's expression of sympathy. She kept the bouquet for weeks, cutting the stems everyday and putting them in fresh water. I was greatly humbled by that experience and discovered it is not so much the gift but the act of giving. To this day, I wonder how sometimes flowers can last so long, especially when they truly have a mission to ease someone's pain.

Over the years I have had some beautiful climbing flowers. Among them are the heavenly blue morning glories growing up the porch posts or over the mailbox or along the split rail fence. And for years I grew scarlet runner beans on the porch posts and everyone kept asking, "What are these?" and "Can I have some seeds?" I was very happy to share the seed pods with them. Sweet peas are another climber which are always favorites of older ladies or of people who remember their grandmother growing and liking them. They are so sweet smelling, delicate, and come in pretty colors. When I am out picking or weeding, and customers sometimes stop to tell me, "My grandmother always grew sweet peas for their wonderful scent," or "My mother loved the colors of cosmos and had them on the dining room table all summer." Flowers certainly help people make connections and conjure up memories and lend themselves nicely to conversations. Flowers also hold special meaning for people because they relate them to people or events in their lives.

My mother loved morning glories (affection) and sweet peas (departure). She wallpapered her bedroom in heavenly blue morning glories. She also liked English ivy (marriage) and wallpapered the living room with an ivy pattern, which helped to camouflage the unleveled walls. Morning glories, sweet peas, and English ivy—all growing on vines. I wonder what that says about my mother's taste in botanical plants?

Helen Coll

My maternal grandfather Woodbury loved peonies (bashfulness, shame) and had a field of them. Each year he would place them in church in memory of his wife, my grandmother, and have them in his real estate office in large Chinese vases. He also grew giant dahlias (instability). What does that say about his personality I wonder? He was a man who liked big, showy things such as large furniture, vases, and flowers. At one time he purchased a huge mahogany, Chinese-style cabinet, that was ornately carved and had ivory inlay. It was so large it had to be cut down to fit in his office.

My father liked forsythias and had a long row of them planted on top of a hill at the edge of a field. What a spectacular sight each early spring when they bloomed their bright, cheery yellow flowers. They were gorgeous and people would take a ride just to see them blooming. Daddy also liked rhododendrons and azaleas. The nursery business owned land in northwest New Jersey where they grew fields of rhododendrons, and in New York state they had Christmas trees growing on land they owned. In Wyckoff the nursery fields had peonies growing by the acre. My brother Edward pulled his little red wagon along the rows of peonies and pulled out all the white stakes identifying the color and variety of peony. Well, when the adults discovered what this five-year-old had done, it was very upsetting, for they would have to wait a year until the peonies bloomed again, to mark them and be able to sell them. He was in deep trouble for some time! Another incident involving young Edward was the time he dug a deep hole with a shovel our Uncle Fred had given him. It was one used by soldiers to dig a fox hole or trench to hide in. It was short, so a man could carry it on his backpack and made of very strong metal. It was just the right size for Edward and did he love to dig holes with it. This one particular hole was very deep and in our grandfather's backyard, and he was not happy when he discovered it, for someone could have broken a leg by stepping into it. The worst incident Edward was involved with was when he set part of the nursery on fire! My father was on the fire department and got a call to put out his son's fire in his own nursery! All this before Edward turned six years old.

Along with growing flowers I have always wanted to commercially grow herbs. At one time I had an herb garden growing, but after a few years it was dug up for a new entrance to a garage. It was nice to have a garage to park my car in after thirty years, but the herbs were gone. I then planted four barrel halves with herbs right alongside the door to my kitchen. One has perennial herbs and the other annual ones. They do very well there and they are so handy to the kitchen for cooking, salads, and garnishes. In the annual barrel I have parsley, basil, and dill. In the perennials I have thyme, tarragon, mint, oregano, and chives. The mint tends to choke out the others, but I keep digging it up, giving it away, and replacing it with other plants. In separate, very large clay pots I have my rosemary bush, as she must be brought in for the winter, and a sage plant. One more barrel half is needed to grow a better supply of various thymes. These herbs are picked for culinary purposes and for bunching to hang from the old, open-beam ceiling in my kitchen and also to include in flower arrangements. I enjoy giving small bouquets of herbs to special friends for the herbs each have individual meanings. Rosemary is for remembrance and is especially nice to use when roasting meats and in salad dressings. Parsley means useful knowledge, feasting or festivity and may be used in almost any dish but is essential in stuffing and potato salad. Sweet basil means good wishes and is a must for every tomato dish. Thyme means activity and is marvelous with fish, chicken, and in salad dressings. Tarragon is wonderful in vinegar and dressings. Mint stands for virtue and, of course, is used in teas, lemonades, and with lamb. Marjoram means blushes and is wonderful in salads and with meat dishes, especially if they have tomatoes in them. Sage means domestic virtue and is good in stuffing, but my husband does not tolerate it well so I grow it for its beautiful foliage, which I use in arrangements. It has velvety, greyish leaves with many veins in them which add a nice accent to any bouquet. Chives are wonderful in any egg dish and in salad dressings, and I like to use it as a garnish for many dishes. When it is blooming, the pretty, round, spiky, lavender blossoms are marvelous in arrangements. I no longer desire to grow herbs for the farm stand because my husband can buy them in the produce market. Caring for and picking herbs was always and still would be, "the job that never got done."

Picking is for me a wonderful time for accomplishing some of my most productive thinking. The cool, early morning, the birds singing their hearts out and flitting around the garden, the beauty that is all around me, such as geese flying overhead in V formation honking their way along the blue sky, the wide wingspan of the hawks swooping, circling, and diving in the fields looking for field mice, even the bees buzzing from flower to flower are music to think by, and the dew drops on the many-colored blossoms are each a photo in the waiting. It is a lot of work but still even more pleasure. What a way to earn money!

Did you know that the more you cut in a cutting garden the better it becomes? Cutting the dead flowers, as well as the good ones, encourages more growth, as all the nutrients and water will then go to the new blossoms. Consequently, each year the ends of the rows nearest the stand, where I begin to cut, always have the best blooms. I feel the same can be said for life; getting rid of the old or dead parts allows for new ideas and growth to take place. I never went to school to learn about growing, cutting, or arranging flowers, not that I haven't thought about it many times. I learned from family, experience, friends, and the cooperative extension people. Over the years my husband and I have learned much by attending extension meetings, be they about poultry, vegetables, strawberries, or cut flowers. The arranging I have learned by doing. My advice is: think in threes (or odd numbers), turn the arrangement often, add unusual flowers or greens for more artistic interest.

One day as I walked into the garden to pick, I encountered an unusual sight. There, in the row I was proceeding down, was a thin snake trying to eat a large frog. Only the head of the frog was in the snake's mouth, the rest was hanging out. I did not want to disturb "the balance of nature" or the "chain of life" (pecking order) and so I went back into the stand to work and at intervals came out to view the progress. A little at a time the snake was able to get more of the frog's body into his own. Finally I came out and they were both gone! I had never seen that before or since, and it was an amazing sight.

An occupational hazard of picking flowers is the many bees I encounter each day. The garden is alive with their buzzing, flying bodies. I do not bother them and they leave me alone; a wondrous respect. Speaking of respect, we need each other, the bees and I. The bees need the pollen from the flowers, and I need the bees to pollinate so I will continue to have blossoms. Each growing season I only get stung one or possibly two times. What happens is this: I am picking in the rain or just after a rain, and the bees are on the underside of the flower petals trying to keep dry but I do not see them there. I place my fingers under the head of the blossom to hold it with my left hand while cutting the stem with my right hand. When I touch them, they sting me in self-defense. The bite stings for a time but generally stops soon. Very rarely do they leave a stinger in my flesh.

All in all, my life "In the Garden" is a marvelous life. I often think about why and how I find myself doing the work I do. Is it in my "blood?" Is it what I am familiar with and comfortable doing? So often people find themselves living lives so familiar to them, carrying on a family image, occupation, ambition. I thoroughly love flowers and I am so happy they bring so much joy to my life. Ralph Waldo Emerson once said, "Earth laughs in flowers."

Cultivating Life
A Story of Earth and Hearth

Left: Flower bouquets for sale—1998.

Below: Helen picking flowers—1996.

Helen Coll

CHAPTER FIVE

CALVES AND HORSES, SHEEP AND GOATS, CHICKENS, DOGS, AND CATS

"All creatures great and small...the Lord God made them all."
Cecil Frances Alexander 1818-1895

It was cold and rainy, not the kind of day for a newborn to be out, when my father came to the house and asked if the kids could come and help him find a calf that had been born in the pasture during the night. Our two oldest children, Suzanne (5) and Mark (3), went with him and sure enough they found the small, black-and-white Holstein calf. Their Grandpa said they could keep her. He gave them a calf feeding pail, one with a large nipple on the side for the calf to nurse from. Each morning and evening the powdered (milk) calf starter formula had to be mixed with warm water for the calf to drink. Soon after, another cow calved in the pasture and they again went with Grandpa to find it. This time it was an orange-brown Guernsey calf. Now that they each had one; Suzanne called her Holstein calf Holly, and Mark named his Guernsey Ginger. They were the first cows we owned.

Suzanne has always loved cows. She would go to her grandfather's barn and help him with the chore of feeding and milking his large dairy herd. She would "hoe down the cows," meaning hoeing the manure into the gutter cleaner which was then run by electricity to remove the manure from the barn. She also picked up the towels that were used to wash the cows' udders prior to the milking machines being placed on them. From the time she could walk she was in the barn with Grandpa helping out. She was so little next to some of the huge Holsteins, but she loved them. White Socks was her favorite and she would be placed on her back by my father. One day she left the farmhouse wanting to go to the barn to see Grandpa and the cows; I checked out the back window to see if she had gotten there okay, and what did I see but Suzanne stuck in the mud. Literally, she had walked in the soft mud with her barn boots and apparently liked the feel of stepping in the mud over and over in the same spot, until she finally was truly stuck. She was enjoying herself and remained calm while being extricated. My father had a very difficult time pulling her out. The only thing to do was let her boots come off her feet and then we dug them out afterwards. She gave us some good laughs over that episode for awhile.

Cultivating Life
A Story of Earth and Hearth

Suzanne and Mark raised Holly and Ginger who were bred and had calves. Once the calves were weaned, Archie had to milk Holly and Ginger. He tired of that chore and so we slaughtered one and then the other in about six months. We purchased a 16-cubic-foot freezer to put them in. Our own homegrown meat and it was delicious! Over the years we continued to raise our own beef and added pigs and lambs and, of course, the chickens. Eventually we purchased another 16-cubic-foot freezer to hold all the meat. After Holly and Ginger and their offspring were gone, we bought four calves through an ad in the *New Hampshire Market Bulletin*. That is a weekly paper anyone can subscribe to by mail, which contains a column by the state commissioner of agriculture, market prices of local commodities, and want ads and for sale ads. At the time we had a Volkswagen van and we drove it to transport the calves. Imagine this van with seats removed and four calves and three kids all in the back! It was something to behold. A few days after we got them, one of the kids came running to tell us one of the calves was down on its side and with its stomach all swollen up. It had bloated for some reason, possibly from its diet, and Archie and I quickly tried to relieve its distress but it died. It was a traumatic scene for all of us. There was so little we could do for it, and it was gone so fast. Many years later our granddaughter Whitney had a donkey, Franny, and it too died from bloat. It was a sweet animal and a sad loss. Now we no longer raise our meat, not since the children left home, and I no longer do canning and freezing of foodstuffs. Our two sons now raise their own meat and sometimes we eat some of theirs.

We named all of our cows—some were bulls and some were heifers. One bull, Jose', got himself into an awful mess one day. Up in the field there was an old well we did not use that was surrounded by rocks, trees, and dense brush. None of that stopped Jose' from exploring, and he ended up falling through the rotted, wooden cover into the well. When Mark discovered him, he came running through the field to the house yelling, "The bull's in the well!" I told him to go get his Dad, which he did, and Archie came to investigate the scene. He then got the tractor and a chain to pull him out. Jose's head was at the top and the rest of his body was down in the well, so Archie put the chain around his neck and hooked it onto the tractor draw bar and told me to drive the tractor very slowly. Mark started to cry, "You're going to choke him." Archie said, "Would you like me to give him a pull and try to help him to get out or should I just leave him there?" Mark said he should help him. With the tractor pulling slowly Jose' was able to get his front feet out and very gradually he was able to get totally out. Well, he was one very happy and grateful bull! He was all wet and kept rubbing his body against us and licking us with his rough tongue. He couldn't get close enough to us and he seemed to be thanking us for saving him. The following week I heard a noise in the back pantry off our kitchen and when I went to look. There was Jose' in the house! He was still so thankful to us he wanted to be with us. After this episode he would come up to the window of our dining room and place one of his huge eyeballs on the window and watch us eat. Eventually he went the way all cows on our farm did—into the freezer and onto our table. Friends thought we were terrible to eat our animals, especially after naming them, but that is the way of farm life and we never questioned it. It was a fact of life for us and provided us with good nutritious food.

Another bull story happened on Gap Mountain in Troy, New Hampshire, a neighboring town of Jaffrey. My father pastured dry cows and young stock there for the summer. We would "check on them" anytime we were on our way to Keene, to tell Daddy they were all there or which ones we saw and which were missing. One day the cows did not come when we called them to the fence by the dirt road. So Archie and Mark, who was about four years old, climbed over the fence to go look for them. I remained on the roadside with Suzanne and Peggy. Archie and Mark walked into the small open field and we were all calling the cows. Some cows finally came, and before long a bull came out of the brushes, charging towards Archie and Mark. We girls screamed to them, and Archie scooped up Mark under his arm and ran "like hell" to a large boulder, and literally flew up onto the boulder just before the bull could get to them. We all gasped with relief they had made it up there, and then laughed at the sight of the boys up on the rock and the bull walking back and forth. We had to wait him out. Finally, he walked away back into the bushes from where he came, and the boys made a mad dash for the fence, which we held apart for them to get out. Then we really collapsed with laughter at the close call.

A few years later when Dave was a young man, he had a bull he was raising for meat, and he was pastured close to our house. One day, unbeknownst to me, the bull broke out and was in the yard. He spied the swing set and slide, where the grandchildren played, and wanted to play himself. With his horns he butted at the slide until it was almost ripped from the ladder, and then he started pushing on the swing set, which was cemented into the ground. That is when I saw him and ran out to stop him, but the damage was done, and the slide could not be saved. He had mangled and removed the slide and was pushing on the upright bars supporting the set. The swing set never stood straight again but was still more-or-less usable. In the summer of 1998 Dave's daughter (our youngest grandchild), Emily, 5, had outgrown the set, so we removed it. No more tilting swings and monkey bars.

Niekeelia knew he was beautiful. His coat of lamb's wool was pure white and combed, curried, and clipped to perfection. He was ready to go to another county fair and be judged against all the other 4H lambs, brought for the show by their 4H owners. Our second daughter Peggy (8) had spent hours shampooing, combing, and cutting his wool and cleaning his eyes, ears, and face to be perfectly groomed. It was a wonderful time in a young girl's life: daily giving the care needed by a young lamb and getting him prepared for judging. Peggy was an excellent caregiver and justly received many blue ribbons for Niekeelia and Jaytha. Before the 4H lambs, Peggy and her little brother Dave each had a lamb, one named Fuzzy and the other Snowball. Because everyone teased about their names, Peggy chose to make up the names Niekeelia and Jaytha for the next two lambs. At the end of the summer the lambs were slaughtered for meat. We love eating lamb and Peggy, an adult now, still does. A few years ago, she and her husband Paul raised sheep for meat.

To exhibit in the show ring at the fairs Peggy had to wear white shirt, pants, and sneakers. It was quite the job to get them white again after a fair, but a small effort compared with the one she had to master to get the blue ribbons. A regret of mine is that my husband and I were too busy with our summer work and the farm stand to make it to most of the fairs. I remember going to one in Keene and one in Deerfield, New Hampshire, and I was very proud of her and her accomplishments. We were fortunate to have another family she could travel with to the various fairs.

Peggy also raised goats. She had a Nubian with beautiful, long, soft ears and a light fawn-and-white fur coat. Goats are wonderful pets and can be trained to do a variety of tricks. They are very much like dogs but need to be fenced or tied in pastureland. Taffy was a good pet and Peggy loved him and cared for him very conscientiously, but he met with an untimely and very sad end. One day he was not in the pasture as usual. Peggy called him and when he didn't come she went to find him. Up in this pasture was an old well, the same one Jose' fell into. We had placed another cover on it but it too was wooden and Taffy somehow fell through a crack in the side and drowned in the well. Archie helped her get him out and together they buried him. A new cement cover was put on the well and it has remained safe to this day.

Peggy wanted another goat so we purchased a young one. He was a black-and-white Nubian. He was fenced in by the old barn across from our farm stand, and customers could see him and pet him. One customer, Edith, an older lady, had raised many goats when she was younger and when she saw our goat was an unaltered male (had not been castrated through the removal of the scrotum, so he could not possibly impregnate a female goat), she told us we would be sorry one day when he was a fully mature male. Well, the day arrived. The goat was now mature and we finally understood what she had been telling us. Did he smell! It was the most awful odor ever and he had to be removed as soon as possible, for the customers did not like the smell at all. Truly, we were in need of immediate action. My sister-in-law, Carmen, told me her cousin's husband would like the goat, no questions asked. The goat was loaded into his trunk and off they went. The next day we received an invitation to a barbecue at his house. Guess who was the featured entree? We declined; who could eat him after smelling that odor! Many years later, Archie and I were in Jamaica and we had curried goat for dinner. It was delicious and on a return visit we ate it again.

Through our goat-raising activities, we found that goats will eat most any vegetation, so you have to be careful where you pasture them. Some plants are poisonous to them, like rhododendrons and mountain laurel, so they must be kept away from them. There was an old saying that goats ate tin cans, but that is not true, they only lick the glue off of the cans.

☺

When our daughter Suzanne was nine, she wanted a horse. She asked and asked, but we did not have the money to buy a horse. A calf or lamb we could purchase for $10-$20 but a horse was $100.00+. A second cousin of Archie's had an older horse, Jesse, and said we could have him for Suzanne by caring for him and feeding him. He was a fine reddish-brown horse. Suzanne took marvelous care of Jesse. We borrowed my brother Ed's western saddle and bridle and Suzanne rode him. She was a good rider and excellent caregiver. Finally at one point in time Jesse went back to his owner and we were able to buy Suzanne a horse of her own. Cricket was a male roan, chestnut color with a white diamond on his forehead. Suzanne was very good and faithful at caring for her horse for several years, but one year, when she was around 13, she lost interest in Cricket. He was not properly taken care of; he was often out of water and feed, and he began to break out of his pasture. He would get into the sweet corn fields and Archie was complaining, mostly to me, and I was nagging Suzanne and nothing was happening except Cricket continued to break out. One day when I was working in the stand Cricket broke out again. A customer helped me put him back in the field. I told him what was happening and he said he would take Cricket off my hands. I was happy to have a solution to "the horse in the corn field" problem in our lives, so I "gave" him the horse. The man went directly home and came back with a saddle and bridle and a young man to ride him to his new home. When Archie came back, I told him what I had done and I thought he would be relieved. He was but he commented, "You could have gotten something for him." I felt I had done the best thing for all concerned and ended the nagging problem for everyone. I didn't tell the kids; I waited for them to notice he was gone. Suzanne finally did notice when she went to the field to give him water and grain, and I then took them to see Cricket in his new barn. We went one more time to see him and then no more. That was the end of horses on our farm.

Cultivating Life
A Story of Earth and Hearth

When I was young, maybe 10 or 11, I also wanted a horse. A neighboring girlfriend had a pinto pony, and one day she said I could ride him. I was doing just fine until we came to a wooden bridge. The horse shied and one back foot went off the side of the bridge. Both the horse and I fell into the brook. Thus ended my riding days; I never had the desire to get onto a horse again.

When Peggy's daughter Lyndsey was ten, she wanted a horse. Archie and I purchased "Thunda" for her, but after a year she too became tired of caring for him and he was sold to a family in Vermont. Lyndsey and her family visited him a couple of times there to ease the loss. If a child is not interested in caring for an animal, there isn't any reason to keep him unless the parent wants to take over the care.

Chickens as pets? Well, no, but as learning experiences they are wonderful. Mark and Peggy were the children that enjoyed raising chickens and turkeys. When they were quite young they had a small coop of hens and a rooster. They cared for them by themselves. One summer we had two young boys visiting from New Jersey, second cousins John and Todd, and they all went up to the chicken coop to check out the chickens. The rooster attacked them using his beak and spurs, and they came running down to the house to tell us about him. Archie asked, "What would you like me to do about it?" and they all said, "Kill him." Archie agreed he had become too old and too aggressive now to be safe for the kids and so he said he would have to be killed. They were excited about the prospect and helped Archie to dress him off, that is remove his feathers and clean out the innards. The next day I roasted him for dinner and John and Todd said he was the best chicken they ever ate. To this day they remember the story and like to tell it to family and friends.

Both Mark and Peggy entered the New Hampshire 4H Chicken of Tomorrow contest and were blue ribbon winners for a few years. Each youngster is given 25 baby chicks to raise for ten weeks then dress-off for the actual judging. They had to keep good records and care for them by themselves. When Archie was a young man he too competed in the same contest. It has since ended due to lack of interest. That is a shame for it teaches young people many lessons and provides their families with good food. One year, when Peggy was ten, she won second place for the entire state. That was an exciting day, for the first and second prize winners were announced last, which meant we were in suspense for quite some time. The first year Mark entered he had the largest and nicest looking pair of dressed chickens, but he won third place because they were not a matched pair. No one told us about that detail, but as we were told by the officials, it is very difficult to judge so many entrants—you have to find something wrong to get the top winners. Mark did participate in a panel discussion in 1972 about the experience of raising 25 baby chicks for ten weeks and dressing them off for the competition. He mentioned he slept in a tent only a short distance from the chicken coop, but it was only because he is an outdoorsman. They learned a lot about raising chickens from day-old chicks to ten-week-old broilers: feeding, watering, keeping records, and finally dressing them off by themselves and choosing two to enter in the state competition. Archie also competed when he was young and in 4H; he won ribbons and learned a great deal from the experience. It was a wonderful foundation for his lifelong career in poultry farming.

Mark also raised 4H turkeys one year, but they met with great misfortune. His entire flock was killed one night by a pack of wild dogs. Our town dog officer, Paul, came and made plaster cast impressions of the dogs' footprints and then petitioned the town selectmen to pay Mark for his dead turkeys. There is an old statute still on the books that says the town is responsible for loss of property due to wild animals. Mark received money for his dead turkeys, and I remember his thinking at the time that it was easy money, for the turkeys were still fairly young, not ready for slaughter, and he had his money already.

Man's best friends also found their way into our lives over the years. When Suzanne was only two years old, we had our first family dog, a purebred beagle named Candy. The first night we brought Candy to our apartment—Archie and I lived in an apartment over his parents' home for the first three years of our marriage—we made a boxed area for her in our kitchen. We gave her a blanket, a toy, and an alarm clock for company. Someone told us the ticking sound would help keep her quiet at night. They supposedly think it sounds like their mother's heartbeat. This was a red leather travel alarm and, you probably guessed it, she chewed the case. It had been a graduation present of mine and I was very sorry to have it ruined, but I realized how foolish it was of me to put it in her pen. For some reason unknown to us, Suzanne started to call her Ringo and so she became Candy Ringo. She was nice dog although very frisky, typical of hounds. Like many dogs, Candy Ringo was one that suffered with gas. Frequently she would embarrass us. She would silently expel gas and we would try to tell visitors it was the dog; they, of course, would wonder if it really were the dog. One evening she met with an untimely death when she was hit by an automobile. I came home from a church women's meeting and there she was, lying in the road approaching our home. Archie had to bury her and in the morning we had to tell Suzanne her friend was gone.

We then moved to our own farm, where we still live today, and a friend's dog had pups and gave us one. It was a "Heinz 57" but looked like a beagle. I do not remember his name but I do remember him by this story. When Suzanne was in first grade she had a pair of tan Hush Puppy shoes. One morning we could not find one shoe. We looked and looked, and finally found it all chewed up. I had to take her to buy another pair of school shoes, and she chose a pair of red leather ones. A few days later one of the red shoes was missing and when we found it, it too had been chewed. Well, as it turned out, the right shoe of one pair was ruined and the left one of the other pair was ruined, and so Suzanne still had a pair of school shoes, only one was red and one was tan. Being on a tight budget as usual, I could not afford to buy a third pair of shoes, and so Suzanne wore the mixed pair to school. I did not think I was doing anything wrong and Suzanne was accepting of the situation. But a few years later, another schoolteacher told me how badly she felt for Suzanne having to wear two different shoes, and that her first grade teacher had Suzanne show her her shoes! I now feel sorry that I made her wear them, but truly I did not think it wrong, and I really did not have the money to keep buying shoes!

The next canine friend was a dachshund named Lady. My father had a friend whose dog had a litter of pups and he wanted the kids to have one. She was finally ready for her new home and so I went to pick her up on Christmas morning while Archie waited at home with Suzanne, Mark, and Peggy. They were all sitting on our raised hearth in the kitchen with their hands over their eyes and were so surprised when we told them to uncover them and they saw Lady. She was such a sweet baby and received a great deal of attention from all of us. She fit into our lives so well. A favorite food she had eaten at her first home I now made her: a soft-boiled egg on toast with a little milk added. She was very pampered. The first beautiful spring day in April, we had her out on our front porch to play. We left her for a short time, unattended, and she disappeared. We searched and searched and called and called, and notified everyone we could think of, but we never saw Lady again. Every time we encountered a dachshund, we thought of Lady. It was many years of looking and making note of each dachshund we saw and then checking for a small scar she had on her side stomach. We were left with a terrible empty feeling and no resolution as to what happened. In a very, very small way I can understand how a parent feels when a child is missing; it is a pain that never ends.

The next canine to come into our lives we adopted from the humane society. It was to be Mark's dog and he got to choose him. He looked like a large beagle and Mark named him Fred. Fred was a good farm dog. He liked to go with Archie early in the morning to pick corn. He was tied the rest of the day but at night and early morning he liked to run. He was a good hunter and watchdog, and we had him for many years. Mark built him a wonderful dog house. One day an adult friend, Chas, was visiting and Fred was in his lap being petted when he suddenly threw up! Well, Chas was so surprised and I was mortified. We were all very embarrassed and it was a long time before I felt comfortable talking about the incident. Another time my friend Pat was sitting by our swimming pool wearing white slacks when Fred ran up to her and jumped right into her lap with muddy paws! Pat still relates the story to friends. Fred grew older and one day when he came back from helping to get the corn, he went into the farm stand and laid down under a table to cool off. A small boy crawled under to pet him and for some reason Fred snapped at him and broke his skin. His mother was very understanding and I told her to take him to their doctor and we would pay for the visit, which they did. Well, this was the second time he had done that. We could not always get to him in time to tie him up when we returned from picking the corn, and he would still be running loose when we opened the stand for business. We now could not trust him any longer. At that time Peggy was seventeen and working at the veterinarian's office; we decided to take him there and have him put to sleep. It was a very sad day but a better ending than if something more serious had happened.

We were then "dogless" for awhile until Dave wanted a dog of his own. He was in seventh grade and kept reading the newspapers for sale ads for dogs. He wanted a German shepherd and finally found one he could afford. On the final day of school in June I picked him up and we drove to Barre, Vermont, to pick out a pup from a litter of seven. It was a long drive, but the price was right and the pups were beautiful. Dave chose a male with a black back. He was a purebred and Dave registered him and gave him the name Duke. Duke was the best dog ever and very intelligent. He grew so fast, though, that he developed hip problems. He would limp from time to time but finally outgrew it. When Dave graduated and moved out of the house, Duke could not go with him and he became my dog. The only times Duke left the farm were his annual trips to the vet; otherwise he was always here guarding the farm and us. Whenever we left for a half a day or so, upon our return he would "tell" us everything that had happened while we were gone. Truly he could modulate his voice and go on and on "telling" us his tale. When he was 12 he developed arthritis and became a house dog. We had to train him to stay in the kitchen or the entry room. I bought him an L. L. Bean large dog bed with a Black Watch plaid cover. At first he would not lie on it, only beside it. Archie was so funny trying to get him to lie on it. He would lie on it and tell Duke how comfortable and nice it was and then try to convince Duke to lie on it. After several months, bit by bit, Duke lay on the bed until finally it became "his place." When he was 14 he became incontinent, first with his bladder and finally his bowels. And so the day came when Archie and I had to take him for his sixteenth and final ride to the vet, where we said good-bye. In deafening silence we drove home with only his collar for comfort. The collar still hangs from a beam in our kitchen as a reminder of an exceptional "best friend." The marvelous sense of security I felt all the years he was with us was now gone, as well as the love, loyalty, and devotion he showed us everyday of his life. I still miss him and I know I would only have another dog on the condition he have the intelligence and faithfulness Duke possessed.

In the 1950s in Jaffrey dog sled races were held in February during the Winter Carnival celebrations. Then there were more dirt roads in the town and we had a lot more snow, so the teams of dogs could race throughout the town. The route they took came down our hill and over the bridge and up the other hill (now Nutting Road). We could watch them from our house. In February 1952 I was invited to a birthday party of a friend and I was to be picked up at the bottom of the hill by the bridge, (the same place we got on and off the school bus each day). While I was waiting, the dog sled teams went racing by. When they reached the bottom of the hill they had to go left, across the stone-arch bridge, and then take a right up the other hill. One team came racing downhill but for some reason the driver never yelled "haw" (which means turn left), so the team went right over the edge of the bridge. The driver yelled "whoa" in time for the sled to remain on the bridge. There the dogs were hanging by their harnesses, until the driver could pull each one back up to the road, and get underway again. Such a sight to see, and it all happened very quickly. I do not know who the driver was, if he won or lost, and I never read about it in the newspaper, so I think he never said anything to anyone. I was the only witness and did tell friends at the party and my family.

Felines also were in our family over the years. The first to arrive was "Pickles," a dark gray, striped, Momma cat. One day the kids came running into the kitchen yelling, "There's a cat in the sandpile, can we feed it?" We fed her and she stayed for years. Great Aunt Jennie called her Vinegar instead of Pickles, but the kids were very gracious and didn't correct her after the first time doing so. We just decided she had two names. She was a good hunter, a good mother, and she had many litters that kept us and friends in cats for several years.

Peggy was the person who cared for the cats. She really loved them and was a faithful friend to them all. Midnight was her favorite cat and she had the record for the most kittens. Peggy has good memories of going to the barn and other buildings "hunting" for Midnight's kittens and then taming them, for they were quite wild from not being near people. Midnight was "left off" here like so many cats through the years. People would no longer want their cat and thus bring it to a nearby farm, where they thought it would be well fed and cared for. Once a cat of Peggy's was missing for several days and we could not find her. Finally I saw her lying on the grass outside the bathroom window. When Peggy came home from kindergarten, Archie and she had to bury the cat. She helped to dig the grave and place the box containing the cat into it. I felt sorry for her having to do that at such a young age, but Archie said she needed to do it and he was there to help. I am allergic to cats, dogs, horses, and other animals, and so all our pets had to stay outdoors, with the exception of Duke in his last two years of life. That made them independent farm animals. They were in and out of the barns and wandered the fields. At present we have Smoky, a beautiful, light gray, tiger cat who happened to appear one day and of course she was pregnant. She has had several litters by now and we have been able to find homes for the kittens by giving them away at the farm stand. There always remains the problem though, of finding the kittens before they become too wild. Smoky is often found greeting customers at the front door of the stand. She meows and they reach down and give her a pet. She is joined by a New Hampshire Red rooster who runs free in the yard. No farm is complete without cats, and we have had and continue to have our share of feline friends, for they help in keeping down the mice and mole population.

One year our grandsons Ryan (10) and Reuben (7) came to live with Archie and me and stayed for eight months. The first day I took them to a man who raised rabbits, and each chose a bunny for his own. They both needed something to love and pet and care for, a positive focus in their lives. Ryan's bunny was white with touches of gray fur and he named her Fluffy; Reuben's was all black and thus named Blackie. They each lived in a cage inside a vacant chicken shelter. When autumn came, one of them ran away and the other burrowed a hole so deep in the shelter that Archie could not reach it way down in the bottom of the hole. We tried and tried to catch it but without success. The boys moved and we forgot about the rabbits until the next spring when Fluffy appeared. He was now a very independent rabbit and came to us sometimes for food and would hop away and remain away for short periods of time. I renamed him Bun Bun, for I couldn't remember his name and it was easier for me to call him that. At this time, Duke was tied out by his house and the rabbit eventually made friends with him and vice versa. Duke, when loose, would chase Bun Bun, who would suddenly stop, and Duke would almost fall over him. He never hurt him. In wintertime I would look out and sometimes catch them lying together to keep warm. Bun Bun would also go to the farm stand and beg carrots from the workers and the customers, then hop away to his independence once again. One year Ryan and Reuben told their younger cousins, Lyndsey and Whitney, "We caught the Easter bunny." The girls were very excited and believed the boys when they saw him in the crate. The girls went to church services that day and told our Pastor, "We caught the Easter bunny this morning." The pastor did not think it true and told me what they had said. I told her it was a fact. We all loved and respected him for five years. Rabbits generally live four to five years. Bun Bun developed arthritis and began to hop slower and slower, and sometimes his back legs did not function properly. One day he hopped away and we never saw him again. He died free as he had lived free. He certainly touched many lives: family, friends, workers, and customers. We all greatly respected him. How I missed that dear rabbit! I now have a collection of rabbit knickknacks from friends and family given to me in memory of Bun Bun, but a dearer pet there never was.

Animals are very important for children to raise. They can learn so many of life's lessons from them—how to be loving, kind, gentle, loyal, and faithful. Animals' needs have to met, such as water, food, exercise, cleaning, and protection, every day. They are dependent on this care or they will die. Children have opportunities to observe birth by watching kittens or calves being born or eggs hatching; they witness mating practices ("Why is that bull trying to ride on that cow's back?"); and they discover death: from natural causes, accidents, predators, and even from our own choices. With raising farm animals they can experience the practical, business side of caring for an animal and what that animal must ultimately sacrifice for them (its life). They learn what went in to producing meat and how to make money doing it. They learn record keeping, and also how to kill and dress an animal for consumption. For all these reasons Archie and I chose to raise our children on a farm and make the financial sacrifices to do so. Farming is a way of life, and our children have benefited from our values and gained very practical knowledge.

"Animals are such agreeable friends—they ask no questions, they pass no criticisms."
George Eliot

Helen Coll

Mark, Peggy, Dave, Suzanne—1969

Dave and Mark—1972.

*Cultivating Life
A Story of Earth and Hearth*

Peggy and Taffy—1972

Suzanne, Cricket, and Dave—1971

CHAPTER SIX

CHICKENS AND MORE CHICKENS

"Here a chick, chick; there a chick, chick; everywhere a chick, chick."
From the song: "Old Mac Donald Had A Farm."

We began our farm with the raising of chickens. We had them five years before we started growing sweet corn and other vegetables. When we first moved here in July 1961, there was a large, old cow barn which had housed cows and horses for many, many years. Archie wanted to raise chickens in it and did some building conversion construction on it so as to house chickens. We first got 5,000 day-old chicks and put them on sawdust covered floors, both downstairs and upstairs. We installed hanging gas heaters to keep them warm. The temperature needs to be about 95 degrees their first couple of weeks for the chicks to survive. For drinking water we had around 80 one-gallon glass water jugs to fill and clean each day. This was before we became more mechanized. The feed also had to be put out by hand into wooden hoppers.

Each day Archie would check the chickens in the early morning before leaving to work with his father on his farm. His Dad was still farming at that time, and because we were not self-sufficient yet we needed the paycheck. During the day I was responsible for checking them both morning and afternoon. Approximately 50 water jugs needed to be filled. I would flip each one over, unscrew the base, rinse it, and fill it with clean water, screw on the base and quickly flip it back again so as to not spill too much water.

I have memories of washing the jugs outdoors before the baby chicks were to come. I was surrounded by dozens of gallon jars and their plastic bases. Sometimes my hands would be so cold I couldn't feel them. I was very happy when the chicks were large enough to drink from the automatic waterers. They were long, metal troughs with a water hose attached to them and a float valve to regulate the water level. These too needed cleaning at least twice daily but not filling. The sawdust or shavings from the floor litter would get into them and needed to be scooped out.

Speaking of floor litter reminds me of having to find a solution for Peggy, whom I had to take to the barn with me because she was too young (1-2) to leave alone, and I couldn't hold her and work at the same time. She could not stand very long and would plunk herself down in the manure and litter and get very dirty. I finally got her a walker to sit in so only her feet got dirty. No wonder she developed a liking for chickens; she was with them so early in life she never has had any fear of them.

The grain came into the building by bulk delivery. When we began our own farm in 1961, bulk grain bins had already replaced grain bags for larger-consumption operations. I was very thankful for that because I would not be able to lift them. It was difficult enough to open the hopper and fill pails and then in turn fill the feeders. Eventually we had automatic feeders with augers to put the grain out. Archie was even more pleased with bulk grain. For so many years all grain came in 100-pound grain bags, all of which had to be loaded and unloaded by hand, one at a time. Archie was always very strong and has a good back from all the lifting he does! Bulk grain meant the grain came in large tank trucks with augers for unloading the grain directly into large bins or tanks on the farm. A tremendous labor saver.

When I was a young girl living in New Jersey, my great Aunt Jennie had a chicken farm and she would get grain in pretty, printed grain bags as well as the usual burlap variety. The printed ones cost more though. My mother would make curtains and clothing from the colorful, printed bags. One summer, when I was about 11, we visited Aunt Jennie and looked at what empty bags she had. I saw one with a beautiful brown, aqua, and white print on it and asked for it. I wanted to make a sundress from it. It would require two bags to make it, so I had to wait and see if she could get another just like it the next week. She was able to get two alike and I made the prettiest sundress I ever saw. It had a wide band around the bodice, bare shoulders with wide straps, a full, gathered skirt, and two pockets on the front. I sent away for the pattern from our local newspaper. Grain bag clothing and curtains "wore like iron." They lasted and lasted, and I never saw anyone with the same dress or skirt as the ones I was able to make. They were a "good thing" (as Martha Stewart says) that today we no longer have.

The chickens we raised were called roasters. We had them for 12 weeks and then they were sold to a poultry dealer that would take them to a dressing plant. Archie's Dad was still in the poultry business and was trucking live poultry to the New York City Live Poultry Market every week from various contract farms he had. The contract farms were owned and operated by individuals, but Archie, Sr. placed chickens in their buildings and paid all expenses (chicks, grain, electricity) and also paid them for their labor and rent for the buildings. Archie would drive the truckloads of chickens down to the city market on Sunday evenings for the Monday morning market sales.

One night he started out driving to New York City, and as he got to Connecticut the famous big blackout of 1965 happened. There was an enormous power failure throughout the Northeast and Ontario, Canada, that night. It lasted thirteen hours in New York City, from November 9-10, and was caused by a malfunctioning relay device near Niagara Falls. He said it was so strange to drive without any streetlights, stoplights, or lighted signs. He felt like he was in another world, a dangerous world, and he did not know what had happened until much later.

Another night I went with Archie on the poultry truck to the New York market, and the following day we went to the World's Fair of 1964 in New York. We worked the day we left and then drove to New York City that night; we could have slept for a couple of hours but I was too excited and busy looking around, taking in this new experience. In the morning, after viewing the market, which was alive with sounds (chickens squawking, men shouting, trucks coming and going) and visiting with business associates (in their tiny offices which were noisy and where we were always being interrupted by someone wanting something), we went to one of the small, Jewish kosher stores. There our live chickens were chosen by the customers from wooden crates, then blessed by a rabbi and butchered at the time of sale. For the remainder of the day we attended the fair. I remember going on a wonderful ride called "It's a Small World"; it later became a feature ride at Disney World in Orlando, Florida. The tune "It's a Small World After All" played in my head for days. We also saw Michelangelo's *Pieta* (the Virgin Mary mourning over the dead body of Christ) which was there on loan from the Vatican. It was a thrill to see it after waiting in line for so long. The fair was very exciting with many rides and foods of all kinds, but we had to leave too soon, for we were tired and had to drive home that evening. We arrived back at 2 A.M. When we came up the hill and into our driveway, we heard a great commotion in the barn. Archie went to check on the chickens and the reason for all the noise. He found there was a skunk in with them. He proceeded to chase it and finally had to kill it with a hammer, the only weapon available. When he came back to the house, did he smell!! I told him, "You can't come in this house." He had to undress on the porch and put his clothes in a plastic bag. He then came in and I went to the cellar and to get some of my homemade tomato juice, which he took a bath in. Such an ending to our World's Fair adventure! The next morning I washed his shoes in tomato juice and his clothing we burned.

After raising chickens in the old barn for nine years, we decided we needed a new, modern building to increase our flock size. Archie's Dad had retired by now and we were farming full time on our own place. In 1971 we built a new 34' x 170' "state of the art" cage laying house for 20,000 birds. On Sunday, November 21 (also my birthday), we held an open house in observance of National Farm-City Week. About 200 plus people came, and we gave each one a dozen box to fill with eggs that they picked themselves from the belts that ran in front of the cages. We served our own sweet apple cider and it was a fun day for all. At the present time this building has been converted to a growing house. We place day-old chicks in it and grow them there for twenty weeks. Then we move them to other poultry buildings where they will lay eggs for approximately one year. It takes 20 to 25 weeks for a chicken to be mature enough to lay an egg. The buildings they are moved into are all free-roaming buildings, completely automated in 1992. At present we have capacity for 50,000 birds. The chickens are on floors with free choice of water, feed, nesting boxes, fresh air, and sunlight; the manure is cleaned out twice daily, and the egg collection is done twice daily. The laying hens are no longer kept in cages. Our operation has evolved many times: we started with chickens, free-roaming on the floor, went to cage buildings, and now are back to free roaming floor chickens, once again. Cage buildings have individual cages that hold four chickens, and are stacked three high and end to end in long rows for automation of feed, water, and egg collection. We now produce natural eggs that we label Nest Fresh 'n' Best which are from chickens fed a balanced diet of pure grains, no animal fats, animal by-products or antibiotics added. We also produce organic eggs we label Pilgrim's Choice from chickens free to roam in protected buildings, on the floor, with free choice of certified organic grain, free of any pesticides, herbicides, chemical fertilizers, animal fats or by-products, and antibiotics. Archie created this niche market several years ago, and we have been able to survive very well in a market system geared for million-bird farms. We believe we are providing people with the best egg possible and under the best conditions possible. Our production is solely brown-shelled eggs.

The old original barn on the farm was built in three stages. The center, or oldest part, was 30' x 30' and to that in the early 1900s was added another 30' x 30' end, and a final wing was added in the 1940s. In the center section, the cows were on a wooden floor and it had rotted. That section was post-and-beam construction while the rest was not. In the 1950s a man cut through the major cross-tie beams to allow for hay bales to be stored on the top floor. Previously the hay had been put in loose and the beams did not interfere, but now they wanted bales to fit and thus cut the beams. This made the roof sag and become weak. Archie did try to tie it together with cables and then cleaned out the rotted floorboards and put in a concrete floor, but it continued to sag at the roof and bulge at the sides. When we built the new building in 1971, we decided it was time for the barn to be taken down. We sold it to a man for the dismantling of it. He could have all the wood and beams for taking it down. While it is true we miss the old barn, it certainly opened up our view of the farms across the way and of our fields.

Throughout the years the breeds of chickens we raise have also changed. We started with roasters that were White Rocks; that is a heavy meat bird, bred for broad breasts and a rapid growth. The laying hens have been various crossbreeds and sex-link chickens. We have had Barred Plymouth Rocks crossed with New Hampshire Reds and other breeds, as hatcheries have developed them. We look for a breed that produces excellent quality, brown-shelled eggs, large in size and with high production rates. The average laying hen produces about 250 eggs per year.

I just realized I have something in common with hens; I, too, have a "nesting" instinct. Plunk me down somewhere and I start to make a "nest," in other words, I make everything around me feel comfortable, homey, be it on vacation, camping, or visiting. I have a need to make a "nest" the same way a hen does for herself and her brood.

One day in the farm stand two ladies were looking inside a box of eggs, which happened to be small eggs, and Archie overheard one of them say to the other, "Look at these eggs. Someone picked them too soon," a funny but ridiculous statement. At this time we have a variety of chickens running loose around the barnyard and the farm stand, and customers certainly enjoy watching them. We have one New Hampshire Red rooster who follows me and sits outside my study window and crows anytime of the day he wants to. He is very funny, as his tail feathers are mostly missing, probably from grandchildren trying to catch him.

Back in the days when Archie and I were dating I would sometimes help him pick eggs on the weekends. I had to learn how to put my hand under the hens so as not to be pecked. Boy, that could hurt and sometimes they would draw blood from the back of my hand, and then they really wanted to peck me. If a hen sees blood she will peck and peck, be it on a hand or on another chicken. My first friendship ring was a red plastic leg band for a pullet. These would be placed on the legs of pullets for identification purposes. I remember one particular time I was reading a book called "The Egg and I" written by Betty McDonald, while Archie was working, and I was laughing so hard I had to try to compose myself long enough to read some of the funnier parts to him. What a marvelously funny book with a great title. I have often been sorry it had already been taken, for it would be perfect for this book. Little did I know that was only the beginning of a lifetime with Archie and with chickens.

As I've been saying all through this chapter, "The only sure thing in our operation is change."

> "The gatherer can always tell
> Her well-turned egg's brown sturdy shell,
> As safe a vehicle of seed
> As is vouchsafed to feathered breed."
>
> Robert Frost

CHAPTER SEVEN

ROCKS, TREES, BIRDS AND BEES

> ""These rock formations," explained the guide, "were piled here by the glaciers."
> "But where are the glaciers?" asked a curious old lady.
> "They've gone back, madam, to get more rocks," said the guide."
>
> Anon.

In the springtime each year there comes a day when Archie announces it is time to "pick rocks." Sounds like they grow and now are ready to pick. I have often heard people say, "rocks don't grow" but it has been my experience through the years we have farmed, that maybe, just maybe, they do. Each year we pick and pick tractor bucket load after bucket load, dumping them in huge piles at the edge of the fields or putting them into large bins to sell, and next year there are just as many or more to pick again. Where do they come from? I know the ground freezes and thaws and heaves the rocks up to ground level, but it truly does seem that they grow!

Part of our driveway is not paved and on any given year it is smooth and the next year a small rock protrusion is noticed. For a few years it slowly becomes a larger and larger bump, until one year we realize it is causing problems. A day will come when Archie or Mark will be driving through the driveway and feel it is time to dig up that rock. This happens over and over. Sometimes it is a simple task but at other times the small peak is attached to a sizable rock. On many occasions the rock is removed after considerable excavating. Then a truck load of dirt must be brought in to fill the hole left by the removal of the rock. On one occasion, I remember the rock was too large to get out and had to be buried again and the driveway graded up around it to make it level with the peak. Sometimes in the spring when the ground thaws and the April rains come, small sink holes appear around rocks and they eventually must be removed or covered.

In the bottom front field there is a large rock, that each year Archie tried to move, but without any success. Well, the year came when a major improvement of the field was taking place, and the rock must be moved. My brother, Ed, came with his large bulldozer and he dug and plowed, and dug and plowed, until there was a huge hole all around the rock, which was now revealed to be a boulder. He tried over and over to push it out of the field but the boulder was larger than his bulldozer and it would not budge. There was only one solution—bury it up again. At times like that, you know you either use dynamite or give into mother nature and let her win.

One sunny day I was fixing lunch when Archie came in and asked me, "Hold out your hand." When I did he placed a heart shaped, flat stone, about one and one half inches wide in it, He had picked up in our driveway, on his walk up from the stand. Such a find—a wonderful token of his love. I still have it in a fountain on my office desk. In his travels he has found many stones of interest: a gray egg shape with a white line around the middle, two flat gray stones, with perfect circles of white on the surfaces, ones that look like a head or a mouse and so forth. Each time he brings a stone to me it is such a tender moment—he says, "Look what I have found and I want you to have it!"—a reaffirmation of his love. Interesting something so hard and cold can convey such a warm and gentle feeling.

We were vacationing in Hawaii last year (March, 2000) and one of the days we were there, we went to Pololu Valley. On our way to the store that morning we picked an avocado and a lime, which I made into guacamole. Pololu Valley is the northern most point of the Big Island and the road ends at the cliffs. We hiked down, way down, to the black sand beach (black from volcanic ash), along a narrow trail of rocks, dirt, donkey and horse dung. It was very steep and had spectacular views. It was a gorgeous, clear, warm day. The beach was splendid and the waves the best and we had it all to ourselves. We ate our lunch of guacamole, tortilla chips and fresh strawberries. A delicious feast in paradise! Archie kept saying, "We are at the end of the world." We were looking out at the sea and the realization came to us that there wasn't anything between us and China and Japan, except the wide, blue Pacific. The valleys of Pololu are lush, green, beautiful, steep, remote and uninhabited, no roads only trails. The water is turquoise blue and dotted with occasional ships and whales. While walking the beach after lunch, Archie found several objects: a log which now was just a round bundle of fibers and some stones. One, a piece of volcanic rock, black and porous, had the letters A and a backwards C on it. His initials! He kept it and brought it home, much to the chagrin of our friend we were staying with. She told us if you take any volcanic rock off the island you will have bad luck (according to the legend of Pele, Goddess of the volcanoes). She mentioned one person who did so but mailed the rock back, because of bad luck he experienced.

In October one year, we visited Nova Scotia and Prince Edward Island. We went to the Bay of Fundy and brought home beautiful purple stones from the beach. We have brought back rocks and shells from many trips, both in the states and from the Netherlands, Jamaica, Bermuda, St. Thomas, and the Bahamas. The fascination with the beauty of rocks and stones is really in us, as is all of mother nature.

Cultivating Life
A Story of Earth and Hearth

"I think that I shall never see, a poem as lovely as a tree.

A tree whose hungry mouth is pressed, against the earth's sweet flowing breast...

Poems are made by fools like me, But only God can make a tree."

Joyce Kilmer, *TREES*

Something I admired when we moved to our farm was the two, more than 100 year old, sugar maple trees that stood in our front yard. They were beautiful giants; though they were actually two trees, from any distance they looked like one huge tree. They were distinctive every season of the year.

In summer and in full leaf, they provided cooling shade and gentle breezes for our home, as they were only 30 feet away. We had two, extra long, rope swings in them, one of which was a tire swing, and the other was a tall swing which gave really high rides. We had a large board seat on the rope and I could sit on it and hold a child or grandchild on my lap and we could swing together, often with the child facing me, legs on either side of me and we would laugh and sing and swing. Or the children wanted to be pushed by me and they would cry, "Higher, higher", or "Push me high and run under," or "Push me to the sky." They wanted to touch the branches or leaves with their toes, which meant they were as high as they could go. One summer we had two young boys visiting us and they slept in Mark's room, which looked out to the trees. The first night I heard them talking and from the sounds of the conversation they were upset and not able to go to sleep. I went into the room to comfort them and they said, "There is a green and white checkered ghost outside the window." When I looked out all I could see was the twilight and a gentle breeze making the trees appear to be ghost-like. We all had a good laugh about it and then they fell asleep and slept just fine.

Autumn brought brilliant yellow, orange, and red colors to our trees. Naturally the leaves fell and then we had to rake them into big piles to remove. But before we did that we would jump and roll in them and bury ourselves up. We all have many fond memories and actual pictures to recollect the piles of leaves and jumping and covering up; dry, crackly, and fragrant leaves with a smell all its own, and carefree, bliss filled times of togetherness.

In winter the trees were so regal looking when wet snow would stick for a while to the bare branches or they would look like sparkling, crystal chandeliers, when covered with ice.

By late winter and early spring we would tap the maples for their sap to boil and make maple syrup. Each tree could take at least four spigots with a bucket hanging from each one. The sugar content of the trees was very high and so made extra special syrup. I have some wonderful pictures of Archie and Mark (about age three)collecting the sap. At that particular time we collected and sold

Helen Coll

the sap to Charlie Bacon, who was commercially making maple syrup. When Mark was around ten he tapped the trees and collected the sap and boiled it down, outdoors on a wood fire and a homemade metal evaporator pan. It takes 40 gallons of sap to make one gallon of syrup. Now that is a lot of hauling of sap. We did the finishing-off in the kitchen. The sap is boiled until it is reduced almost to a syrup and then must be very carefully watched, so as not to burn it. When it reaches 7-9' above boiling it is pure syrup. By doing the finishing-off in the kitchen we were better able to watch it, monitoring the temperature and regulating the heat more accurately than with the wood fire, but it made for a messy, sticky stove, walls, ceilings, and floor! But, the results were always worth the trouble. Nothing, no nothing tastes as delicious as that sweet, liquid gold that is 100% pure maple syrup from a wood fired evaporator! Today, Mark has a commercial operation with a sugar house and a 172 gallon evaporator, 1500 taps set out, and sells the maple syrup in the maple and gift shop located by the farm stand. He also makes heavenly maple soft serve ice cream, delectable maple candies, and sumptuous maple covered walnuts. Our tourist customers and our regular customers are always looking for 100% pure New Hampshire maple syrup to give as gifts and for their own enjoyment.

In the fall we have many tour bus loads of "leaf peepers" (people out to see the gorgeous fall foliage colors) come to the farm. One year I remember a bus load of Japanese tourists from San Francisco coming to see the leaves. Each one had one to three cameras around their neck and the entire busload bought every container of maple syrup, no matter the size, that we had in the stand. I was told they appreciate different sweeteners and I believe it.

We had a Vietnamese student from Franklin Pierce College who was attending our church come for dinner one night. He tasted some maple syrup and it was love at first taste. He later moved to Garden Grove, California and married. We sent him the perfect wedding gift from New Hampshire—our maple syrup and a pewter pitcher to serve it with.

We had the pleasure of those two maple trees for 36 and 38 years. They began to rot and loose limbs, and the woodpeckers were having a holiday, everyday, pecking in the them. After a storm in 1995 we lost half of one tree and the other half had to be cut down in 1997. We then had only one tree left but it looked like half a tree, because of the way they had grown together. Together they were large and filled out and looked like one tree. In 1998 a large part of the remaining tree broke off and the half left was the closest to the house and it was leaning towards the house. And so in the summer of 1999, on a day that was 95' in the shade, a tree service came and cut down the last of the maples. I filmed it and took many photographs of the operation. It was very sad loosing our giants of summer shade, colorful leaves, snowy branches, holders of swings and maple buckets.

The loss has changed the appearance and exposure of our house so much so I have had to buy shades and awnings for our two, eight foot sliding doors and a four foot picture window, which are all on the south side of house. The windows are wonderful in the winter for their passive solar heating but in the summer we need the protection from the intensity of the sun's rays.

I still miss my trees. Thank goodness I have paintings and pictures of them and many happy memories through the years, but still it is such a big loss. We have planted some young sugar maples but it will be years before we will reap the benefits of their shade and maple sap.

When Dave was less than a year old we purchased a red Norway maple and planted it on the front lawn by our stonewall. Dave is now 33 and the tree is 60 inches around. It took that many years for it to reach that size. I always think about its growth in relationship to Dave's age. Trees are each unique in formation and cannot be replaced, accept through time and care. I have always had difficulty with cutting down a tree, as Archie well knows. We have an old apple tree down in the middle of the front field and for all the years we have lived here, he has wanted to cut it down and I want to keep it. It is so spectacular when it blooms in springtime, but he says that is so short a time out of the entire year. It still stands! Sometimes I am not asked about removal of a tree because my response is probably known and usually it is-no. This past fall several trees were cut down and a stonewall removed, so as to join two fields into one large one. I lost my bittersweet supply with the trees and I wasn't asked about the renovating!

A neighbor across the street from our home in New Jersey had a charming Japanese red maple tree, which I always liked, so when I developed a flower garden outside the sliding glass door of our living room, I planted a very small (all I could afford at the time) Japanese red maple. I have nursed that tree for many years, and finally it is almost as tall as I am. It has required extra special care but that makes it even more precious. It is an astounding focal point of the garden.

One of the most outstanding and unusual trees is a gigantic, old maple, at the property line between our other farm and the Deschenes farm, where the Smallpox Cemetery of 1792 is located. It is probably 200 or more years old. Whether you look at it from north, south, east, or west it looks very different. You can see faces in the tree as well as many structural aberrations.

Also on our other farm Mark as developed a fine grove of sugar maples. He had my brother, Ed, log it for him a few years ago, so as to open the maples to light and give them more space to help them grow and for ease in reaching the trees for tapping and gathering.

Every year for 40 years we have cut our own Christmas tree on our land. Most were balsam trees and three were blue spruce. When the children were

Helen Coll

young we would all set out walking and carrying a bucksaw, to cut the best Christmas tree we could find for that year. We also cut one for Archie's parents, as he had always cut a tree for them since a young boy. Sometimes it was a happy occasion but sometimes, mostly due to cold weather, it was not pleasant or fun. There were tears and complaining in more than one year.

As with most old homes in New Hampshire, we too have a large stand of lilac bushes, located on the west side of our house. Every spring I cut huge arms full of the purple lilacs to bring the fragrance and beauty into our home. When Peggy was married in May we decorated the church with lilacs. A beautifully scented, lovely lavender color flower head, made up of clusters of tiny trumpet shaped blooms with lush green leaves. It is the official state flower for New Hampshire. Throughout the state many old homes have crumbled to nothing more than a cellar hole, but the lilacs still bloom by them every spring.

My love of trees and shrubs probably comes from my father and grandfather and their nursery/landscape business. My brother, Ed, is at present a logger and really knows trees and different types of wood, and our son Dave left working on our farm to run his own logging business. Sometimes I think these things are in our blood, so to speak, like the love and knowledge of flowers I got from my mother and grandmother.

"Once you have experienced New Hampshire, I am sure that you will agree with me.
The state is a wonderful place for birding and for exploring nature."
Alan Delorey, *A Birder's Guide To New Hampshire*

Now that I have more time than when I worked seven days a week and long hours, I have put up several bird feeders, which I carefully tend and relish watching everyday, all year long. From both our kitchen and living room sliding doors we can see all species of New England songbirds feeding and interacting. Each year we have one or two gorgeous red Cardinal families, which are my favorites. We also have dozens of adorable Black-capped Chickadees, plump Dark-eyed Juncos, and Purple Finches (the official New Hampshire state bird) as well as House Finches, American Goldfinches, and three types of Woodpeckers (the Downy, Hairy and Piliated). Also feeding are the iridescent Blue Indigoes, cute Nuthatches, rosy colored Mourning Doves, sassy Blue Jays, hungry Evening Grosbeaks as well as colorful Rose-breasted Grosbeaks, tiny Vireos, dashing Red-winged Blackbirds, Rufous-sided Towhees, proverbial American Robin, and many, many more.

Of course feeding the birds brings the chipmunks, red squirrels, gray squirrels, and the occasional skunk. In a base cabinet in our kitchen, one year, we heard awful gnawing sounds and when we looked inside there was a gray squirrel. He had chewed a large hole in the back of the cabinet wall. We tried to get him out but not with any success, so Archie had to shoot him right there. Such a mess! We have had other times when squirrels have gotten in the walls and they not only make a lot of noise but they do a lot of damage. I have trapped so many red squirrels and chipmunks, all of which I take for a long car ride and let them go in wooded areas. They truly are pests of the first order.

While cleaning house one day I heard a noise in the dining room. It was a squeaky kind of cry. I looked and looked but could not find anything. Another day I heard it again and this time I was determined to find out where it was coming from. Walking, waiting, listening; finally I realized it came from the chimney of the fireplace. Well, it seems we had a family of chimney swifts. It is amazing that they can fly straight down and up a chimney. That one summer we had three families in the chimney, and each year we had some more families, until we had some work done on the chimney, and we haven't had any since.

Out of the kitchen window, over my sink, is the view of our swimming pool and beyond it some fields. Many times I have seen flocks of wild turkeys out there. The most I counted at one time was 34 turkeys. On another occasion in the fall, I saw a large bird that looked like a goose and was white. I grabbed my camera and very quietly went out the back door. I kept taking pictures and walking very slowly towards it. I thought any moment it would take flight, but it didn't fly away, it just laid there at the edge of the field. I didn't want to disturb it anymore so I went back into the house. I continued to watch it each day for about five days, and one day it was gone. It apparently had recovered from its injuries enough to fly away. I looked up what kind of bird it was and it turned out to be a snow goose.

Speaking of snow, way back when we were raising chickens in the upstairs of the old barn, Archie had gone to a Farm Bureau Federation convention in Monterey, California, I went to check the flock and found something was really distributing the chickens. I called a friend, Andy, and he came to my rescue. He shot what was causing the trouble and it turned out to be a snowy owl. It was so sad that he was shot (I still feel badly about it) but we had to protect the remaining chickens from piling up and suffocating themselves.

A favorite sight and sound of mine are the Canada geese, both arriving in the spring and leaving in the fall. I love to here their honking and see them flying in their V formation. They like to land in our cornfields and often we see them blanketing the fields with their hungry bodies. Also in the fields we see Killdeer. They make their nests right in the soil amongst the rows of vegetables. When they see us coming they start to screech and stagger in a fake, broken wing, dance to draw us away from their nest. The nest are well camouflaged but very vulnerable to feet as well as tractors. It seems they could find a better place for their nest but it is their nature to place them there. Other field birds we see many of are: of course the Black Crows, Common Ravens and Hawks of many kinds. Many years ago Archie's father would put the chickens out on ranges (open fields) for the summer and I remember once seeing a Hawk dive down and pick up a squawking chicken and fly away with it. Such a helpless sight to behold.

Each year we have Hummingbirds fly inside the greenhouses, where we have our sales area for flower plants and about a hundred hanging plants. They are mostly attracted by the red and orange flowering plants. But sometimes they fly inside the farm stand, which is connected to one of the greenhouses. When this happens it causes a great deal of alarm for the customers as well as the clerks. No one wants the Hummingbird hurt, but it swoops and dives and scares everyone. Usually we leave them alone and they eventually fly out in their own time.

Earlier I told the story of the children being shot at by a hunter, while playing in their tree house at the edge of the field by our house. That was the first tree house Mark built. When he was a little older he built another, a two-story tree house, nailed between four pine trees, out in the woods and quite a distance from home. It was cleverly constructed; a large, comfortable tree house—an early glimpse of his talent with construction. When he was 26 he designed and built his own contemporary cape home with passive solar heating and main heating from wood fired stoves. It is a unique looking house that is very homey and comfortable with a grand view of both of our farms and Temple Mountain range and Pack Monadnock.

> "How doth the busy little bee improve each shining hour,
> And gather honey all the day from every opening flower."
>
> Isaac Watts, *Against Idleness*

Bees are crucial to growing vegetable and flowers. Bees feed their young a mixture of pollen and honey. They depend entirely on flowers for their food, which consists of pollen and nectar (honey). Bees go from flower to flower gathering pollen. They are of far more value as pollinators than they are for their honey or wax production. The flowers on vegetable plants need bees to make fruit grow. If we have a raining period and the bees can't work, I have very few flowers to pick, for the bees haven't been able to pollinate them. We haven't gotten into the bee business (apiary), we rely on others to put their hives around the edges of our fields. As I stated before, each flower picking season I usually get strung once or twice but fortunately I am not allergic to them. It can be very serious, life threatening, for those who are allergic.

Our children would play with matchbox cars by the hour, up the dirt road from our home and stand. That is, they made farms and towns and used mosses and twigs to landscape them, by the old stonewall. They would make miniature communities to the scale of the matchbox cars, trucks, and tractors. This activity would occupy them for hours on end and it was nice for me, as I knew exactly where they were playing.

Also along that stonewall there were places where blackberries were growing. On one particular day, Peggy was picking berries with her brother and sister, when she apparently disturbed a yellow jackets nest. They all came running and screaming to me and I carried Peggy into the house, and found her body covered with bites. I quickly removed her shorts and shirt and put her into a bathtub of cool water, made a paste of baking soda and put it on her bites. It took awhile but she fully recovered. I was thankful she was not allergic and that she handled the experience so well, for it could have had another kind of outcome.

Our lives are continually dictated by the weather and the seasons. It is one of the best reasons to live in New England-for the seasons and constantly changing weather patterns. When someone complains about the weather here, people will say, "Just wait and minute, and it (weather) will change." Here we have five seasons: spring, summer, autunm, winter and the "too" season. It is always too hot or too cold or too wet or too dry!

CHAPTER EIGHT

WATER, WATER, EVERYWHERE?

"O Luxury, extravagant of resources and never satisfied with what costs little...learn how little it costs to prolong life, and how little nature demands...Running water and bread are enough for mankind."
Lucan, DeBello Civili

People in general take for granted such essentials in life as clean air to breathe and water to drink. They are wasteful of these precious resources. How many times do we brush our teeth and leave the water running? How often do we have a faucet that is leaking and do nothing to fix it? Are our showers too long and our tubs too large?

I first learned the value of water when I lived on a dairy farm. Cows each drink 25-30 gallons of water per day. Our wells would become very low in the summertime and the river would be dry, but the cows needed water and so did we. But humans were secondary to the cows. They were our livelihood, essential above all else. We could be flexible in our water consumption needs.

In the summer we did not have water for flushing toilets or bathing. Instead we would go to the barn and get a pail of water from the large, wooden water trough that had water for the cows as they came in from the fields to be milked or as they were going out to pasture after milking. And so, when "mother nature" called, I would head for the barn, a galvanized pail in hand, where I would dip into the water trough for water. Then I would walk back to the house to use the bathroom and flush the toilet with the water in the pail. This was daily procedure throughout the long, hot, dry summers.

Likewise, in the evening several times a week, we would drive to a local lake to swim and to bathe. Sometimes we had to use soap and would do this after dark. We would lather up and then plunge in to the lake to wash the soap off and rinse ourselves clean. I remember fear as part of the bathing necessity: it was dark, and maybe there were snakes in the water. I have a fear of snakes and find myself thinking of their presence at times when I am in the dark. I also have fearful thoughts going into a dark bathroom and sitting on a toilet when I cannot see what is in it—always a snake comes to mind. I must say that I never encountered a snake at night in the water but have during daylight, most likely because I could see them then. I have never seen a snake in a toilet but have heard stories concerning them there.

Cultivating Life
A Story of Earth and Hearth

Outside our creamery room (where the milk was pasteurized and bottled), we had a barrel to collect rainwater from the gutter. This we then used to wash our hair. But if the summer was hot and dry, we would not have water in the barrel and swimming was the hair-washing solution.

Our prayers for rain were always a quandary; on the one hand we needed rain for the wells; on the other we almost always had hay cut and drying and did not want it to get wet. Resignation was the solution. In time it would all be resolved and our hopes were to have both rain and hay that had not gotten wet. For optimum nutrition for the cows from the hay, it was desirable to get it cut, dried, and in the barn without getting wet. As a result of having to guess what weather would be coming our way, we were always (and still are) listening to the weather forecasts. It is a daily question in our home, "Did you hear the weather?" Either Archie or I ask it of the other each day and sometimes twice a day. In spring, summer, and fall we need to know when the rains are coming and sometimes when they will end. Farming is dependent on the weather and what "Mother Nature" or God sends to us. Here in the northeast we are fortunate, for the weather is ever changing. Rarely do we have extended weeks of one weather pattern. Also, we do not have too many devastating weather conditions, such as hail, tornadoes, conditions of extreme dry and heat, and not many hurricanes. We are not totally without disasters, but are not subject to them as much as we hear from other areas of the country. Archie has become a good weatherman. His predictions are better than the TV weathermen being paid to forecast!

Water is a limited resource and we all need to treat it as such. A healthy respect for it needs to be a priority of everyone. Not to have good, clean, clear, healthy water is disastrous for anyone. It is a necessity, should not be wasted, should be cared for by not contaminating sources or using carelessly. It took my experience in childhood on the dairy farm for me to fully respect and appreciate the role water plays in my life. Often I find people do not give the consideration to water it deserves. They think of it as always there, available when they need it, but that may not always be so. Consideration should be given to the use of water, be it from a faucet, in a lake or river, or in the wetlands.

My parents finally had the money to drill an artesian well, and the day came when it was completed. The water was not the best because it contained a lot of iron, but the quantity was wonderful. It was an astounding feeling to at long last have a solution to their shortage of water.

When Archie and I moved to our farm in summer 1961, we had a well 250 feet deep but with only a half gallon per minute flow. It was one of the first artesian wells, made in 1942 by a hammer drill not a rotary drill. For a few years we made do, but one day the children became ill with stomach upsets and diarrhea, which persisted. I had noticed the water did not smell too good at times and so we had it tested. The results were a high bacteria count. We needed to do something, but what? We called a well driller to come and assess the situation, and on his advice we drilled at the same site, hoping to gain a better flow. At 500 feet we told him to stop even though we hadn't gained very much. We could not afford to have him drill deeper. The flow was one and a half gallons per minute. We did not have any further problems with high bacteria, though our water supply for our chickens, gardens, and household had not increased by very much.

In 1971 we built a new poultry building and at the site we had another well drilled. They drilled and drilled for several days. One day at lunch Archie and I were discussing what to do, for they had not struck substantial water flow and were at 220 feet. Should we continue at the same site? Or should we try another site? From our table in the kitchen we could see across the fields to the site while we talked about our options. All of a sudden, we saw a young man running and leaping across the fields and we ran out to meet him. He told us, "We hit water and it is a true artesian." We ran back with him and sure enough the driller said with the pipe he had for measuring the flow that we had at least 50 gallons per minute. That was the best news we ever had! And it was very good water—great tasting and without excessive minerals!

For many years the children and I had wanted a swimming pool, but there was not enough water. When we found this much water, the kids all shouted, "Now we can have a pool!" The following year we purchased a kit for an inground 16' x 32', metal sides with vinyl liner, pool. It was a "do it yourself" project (the only kind we could afford). Archie told us, "Start digging!" and we did, out the back side of our farmhouse in the pasture where there aren't any trees. It was the perfect location for a pool—no trees and a gorgeous view! Mark, who was 12, did most of the digging. He also did much of the cement work in the bottom of the pool and on the walkways. At that time we had an older man, Mr. Bibeau, doing odd jobs for us and he was helping Mark and me with the cement work when he accidentally stepped in the wet cement. He was so surprised and very mad. His black, high-top work shoes were all cement. He spoke English with a French Canadian accent but only said French words in anger about his shoe. We didn't laugh in front of him, but later, when relating the story to Archie, we could hardly tell him the happenings for our laughter. It still brings a smile to me when writing this. A backhoe was needed to finish the project, as there were some huge boulders in the bottom which needed to come out. Each night we read the directions and the following day did the next steps. The only problem arose when we were shaping the hopper for the deep end of the pool and we had one more huge boulder to remove. The backhoe came again and dug it out, and while lifting it up and over the sides of the metal walls, it suddenly swayed and bumped one side. Our once perfect pool now had a very slight curve to that side, but we at last had our pool, complete with a diving board and slide. We have enjoyed it now for 29 years. It has made our summers so much more enjoyable. We have to work long, hard hours and having a pool to cool off in and relax by makes life much more bearable.

Archie never learned to swim until we installed the pool. When he was a youngster, his family was too busy to go swimming and so he never had the opportunity. I, on the other hand, grew up loving the water and swam every day all summer. He still doesn't really enjoy the water but does swim to cool off. He also swims on occasion in lakes and in the ocean. Our four children and eight grandchildren all like to swim and it has provided us with some wonderful social times in our otherwise busy summers.

Our good luck with the new well provided us with more income from the increased number of chickens we could raise, to the water needed for growing more crops. And it gave us pleasure—with a beautiful swimming pool and good tasting, healthy water to drink.

A few years later the town of Jaffrey drilled a well just down the road from our well for use in their new sewer treatment plant, and our flow went down drastically, to only three gallons per minute. We then redrilled our well to 550 feet and now have approximately 13 to 15 gallons per minute. Another side story of water problems we have had over the years was when the town landfill, which was located up the road and across from a duplex house we owned for farm workers or other rental tenants, became polluted with toxic chemicals derived from industrial cleaning solutions. The well is still polluted and has an aeration system installed on it to rid it of these pollutants.

When the power fails, as it does from time to time, and the water pump cannot work, once again we understand what a precious resource water is. Problems come from not remembering its value all of the time. Our animals and pets need water every day both for drinking and cooling down their bodies. They are dependent on us to provide it for them and without it they would die. We too must have water in order to survive.

Water and air are essential to life; without them you cannot live. Respect them, care for them, do not pollute or waste them.

> "When the well is dry, we know the worth of water."
> Benjamin Franklin, *Poor Richard's Almanac*

> "The noblest of the elements is water."
> Pindau, *Olympian Odes*

Helen Coll

CHAPTER NINE

HAZARDS WE ENCOUNTER: ANIMAL (Predators) and HUMAN (Vandals)
a source of danger, obstacle, risk, peril

In the hot, humid summertime, we sleep with the windows wide open, hoping to catch every cooling breeze, and our bedroom is located on the back side of our old farmhouse. Outside the back of the house are several fields. In these fields we grow strawberries and corn, and one is fenced off with turkeys in it. They are 'free range' turkeys, grown for our customers' Thanksgiving dinners, and they live outdoors, pecking the earth for worms and insects. We buy the turkey poults when they are one day old and house them in an old trailer body where they have heat, water, feed, and are protected from predators until they are old enough and big enough to go outside safely.

Getting water up to the turkeys presented a problem. We had an old well in the field, the same one the bull and goat fell into, and after making several tries we were able to pump water from the old well. Electricity had to be brought up to the pump, and priming it took patience. The well now has a safe concrete cover on it—no more wooden covers. The turkeys grew; they were large white ones. At night, through the open windows of the bedroom, we could hear, early in the morning, 2:00-2:30 A.M., the cries of coyotes. They make an eerie sound that startles me awake; I can feel my heart pounding, my stomach is upset, and I am scared.

One morning when Mark went to check on the turkeys and give them their grain and water, he discovered the field strewn with dead turkey bodies. They were large birds with beautiful white feathers now covered with bright red blood. Such a sad sight, it made our hearts ache. There were, at final tally, 35 dead ones. The coyotes had killed them just for the sake of killing! They did not eat them. What a loss and tragedy. To this day I do not know why I did not hear them being killed. Maybe I was too tired and in a very sound sleep. I just do not know.

We called a local trapper we know and he came and was able to trap many of the coyotes. We paid him a bounty for each one caught. One day Mark was able to shoot quite a large coyote. He drove down to the yard with him, dead in the back of his pickup truck. He was a healthy and beautiful specimen: he had a long, thin nose, fur of white, tan, and black, and a bushy tail. I was glad he would not bother us any longer, but at the same time I felt some sadness too.

Cultivating Life
A Story of Earth and Hearth

Mark skinned him and to this day has his pelt hanging on his coat rack at his home.

One night when I heard the coyotes, Archie was home (not up at 2:00 A.M. to go to the Boston produce market) and he got up and looked out our window to see an entire pack crossing the back field. He said there were many, around 25, in the pack. Now that we no longer have our beautiful, intelligent, protective German Shepherd dog, Duke, I have more fear of the coyotes and what they may do. I do not dwell on the insecurity though; most of the time I don't think of it. We have experienced the loss of cats and rabbits from time to time, and usually we attribute the loss to coyotes, but it may not always be so. When returning from picking corn the other day Archie and I saw three large, healthy looking coyotes crossing an already picked cornfield, and last night we again heard them cry, so they are still in our area.

Other wild animal sightings in our area have been of moose, but we have not personally seen them, although one was sighted just up the road from us. This summer a family of five bears were eating our corn. We saw their footprints and the chewed corn cobs and where they had played and slept. They did quite a lot of damage and when the hunting season began for bear, Archie signed a permit for a Jaffrey hunter to go onto our property. The season is only seven days long, but he shot his one allocated bear in our fields. He showed it to us as it lay in the back of his pickup truck. The bear was 255 pounds and measured six feet from nose to tail and was a boar (male), estimated to be three to four years old. Fish & Game officials have had several reports of bears in our area and they have been responsible for not-so-subtle damages. During the seven-day hunt five bears were taken in our area of the state. Last summer a customer sighted a bear crossing the highway towards the river and our cornfields. Predators are a continuing problem for farmers and homeowners.

The turkeys we raise taste so much better because of their diet and outdoor life, but there are many problems to overcome: weather, water, predators. We live our life dependent on nature—unpredictable, cruel, and yet beautiful, every day something new and surprising.

When our children were very young we had a pack of wild dogs that would sleep in our machinery shed, and we would see them running together in the fields and down the dirt road. For a while I would try to keep the children in the house, for I was not sure what the dogs would do. I have heard stories of wild dogs and coyotes attacking young children in their own yards and did not wish to have any unhappy events of our own.

Through the years we have had our share of problems from human troublemakers as well as from animal predators. Animals we can excuse more readily than the human vandals. The following are some stories of the human kind.

One Friday evening Archie and I were in the farm stand taking stock of things for the busy Saturday to come. It was about 8:30 P.M. and the stand was closed when a man knocked on the door. When we answered the door, the man stated, "My Jeep is stuck in some mud or chicken manure and I need help getting out." Well, he had been drinking, he was stuck in a place he didn't belong. It was late for us and we had had a long day and an even longer one coming, so Archie told him to use our phone and call someone to pull him out. The next day Archie discovered someone had driven all over the entire field of White Cloud popcorn we were growing and ruined the crop for harvesting. Now popcorn takes a long season to mature and it would be ready to pick soon, and so that was a substantial loss for us. We called the police and told them about the incident the night before and that we suspected that man may have taken revenge on us for not helping him get out. The police proceeded to go to his home and check out his Jeep. Sure enough they found the wheels and undercarriage full of corn tassel seeds. The police still did not think it enough evidence to arrest him on, so he got away with it. We never grew popcorn again.

One warm summer evening, Archie and I were sitting in our living room when we heard some noises out in the vegetable field across from our house. Archie found his gun and both of us went out to see what was causing the noises, suspecting raccoons or some animal. When we got to the edge of the field, he heard rustling sounds and voices, so he raised the gun and shot straight up into the air. We then heard footsteps running from the field, a motor start up, and a vehicle drive away. The next morning upon exploring the field, Archie found huge, black, garbage bags full of green peppers and cucumbers left in the field. The thieves had done our picking for us, only they picked too many and all sizes, thus some was wasted.

Another evening, this time in the fall, I heard someone out front by the stone wall where we displayed pumpkins for sale. I went to the window of the front door and saw a young man carrying a pumpkin to his truck. I was in my nightgown but forgot that and ran out the door, across our front lawn, yelling at him, "Hey, stop stealing my pumpkins!" He jumped into his old pickup truck and drove off, but I was able to get a good look at him and his truck. I knew his name. The next day I called the police and they came out to see me. I gave them the information, told them who he was, by name, and said I wanted to go with them to his house to identify him. They said I could not go and accuse him, just like that, without any warning! Imagine, he was stealing from me and I could not infringe upon his rights and accuse him! The police did talk with him and he admitted that he was stealing pumpkins from us. The police decided he should clean up the road to our farm, where pumpkins had been smashed. He never did the clean up, but then I never saw him around our farm again either. Over the years pumpkins are what have been stolen from us the most.

Cultivating Life
A Story of Earth and Hearth

Some years we have grown tomatoes in cages, and one particular year that was the case. Our fields are large—we plant hundreds of tomato plants and then put hundreds of cages over them. On driving up the road to the field checking on the crops one morning, Archie discovered someone had deliberately driven over many tomato plants and cages. Just plain malicious damage. There were tire marks but the police never were able to find anyone responsible. Now we stake and tie our tomato plants—no more cages.

Our neighbors down the road called one morning about 2:00 A.M. to tell us a truck had driven by their home into our back fields. That year we had potatoes and corn planted there, and they thought we should come down and investigate what these people might be up to in our fields. Well, we couldn't do anything in the dark, but the next day, when Archie and Mark went out to pick corn there, they found someone had dug up potatoes. They figured about 500 pounds were taken. We were never able to prove who did it and so we had to accept loss.

In autumn one year, Archie was picking corn in a field when shots rang out close by him. It was a hunter shooting at some ducks. It seems the Fish and Game officer had earlier released some ducks for hunters, and he wanted to relaease them where there was a good supply of food for them. Archie then requested the officers check with him each time to see if he had finished picking the fields before released any wildlife in them. Another close call with hunters!

About 20 or so years ago, we had what we called "potato harvest weekends." Archie planted potatoes on the field close to the farm stand, and come fall he would dig the potatoes with a digger pulled by a tractor, and customers would then follow after and pick up potatoes into bags or baskets. We then weighed the containers and sold them the potatoes at a very low price. Everyone seemed to enjoy this activity, but then we found some people were just driving away without stopping to be weighed and paying for them. We finally ended that deal. A local artist, Gil Emery, painted a watercolor of the potato harvest. We have it hung in our farm stand along with one he did of "pick your strawberries," which we also used to do.

At high noon on a hot, 95 degree, humid Sunday; Archie, Paul, and I went to the cornfield to pick more corn for the farm stand. What should we encounter there but two young men picking our corn. Actually they were stealing our corn! Their arms were full and as they walked out of the field to their truck, Archie stopped them and asked, "What do you think you are doing?" They replied, "Someone told us you didn't want this corn anymore and we could help ourselves." Such a lie! Here we are working hard on an extremely hot Sunday and they, being the bums they are, are stealing from us. I spoke to them explaining, "This is how we support ourselves, our families, and many employees, by growing and selling sweet corn. What do you do?" They did not reply. They just dropped the corn on the ground and left in their truck. We proceeded to pick corn and upon returning to the farm stand I called the police to tell them what had transpired. They came up and got the whole story from us and the thieves names, for we knew them both. It was later reported to us that the two young men were in a local convenience store, after leaving the field, bragging about their escapades. As usual, nothing was done about it, they just got away with it.

This past growing year we had another similar experience. It was fall and we were picking the last of the sweet corn in the field farthest from the stand and only accessible by tractor or truck. Paul, Archie, and I were once again the ones picking, and we knew there was just one more day for that field. When we got there we saw someone had driven through the field and ruined the corn. We were very upset and angry. I said we should put out a board with nails in it to try to catch whoever had done this should they come back. Paul said, with tongue in cheek, "We would probably be the ones punished for destroying someone's tires!" We then proceeded to leave when Archie called to me to stop the tractor. He jumped off and went into the field and picked up a New Hampshire license plate. You should have seen the smiles on our faces, for we knew we had them dead to rights with that evidence. When we got back to the stand Archie and I both went to the police station with the license plate and spoke to the person in charge. We thought that he would tell us who it belonged to right then, but no, we had to wait. Well wait we did. We did not hear from the police; I had to call them, twice, and still got nothing but excuses. Finally, after three weeks, I called the person in charge and he said that we did not have enough evidence to proscecute, for the person who owned the truck said someone had taken his plate off his truck and must have lost it there. No matter what proof we have there is never a conviction!

For many, many years we had a self-serve stand in the winter time. People could come to the old stand and get their eggs and cider and leave their money in a box. Some people still remember doing that and mention it to us. Some even brought their visiting friends to show them how trustworthy we are out here in the country. From time to time we did have problems with eggs missing and no money being left for them. One time we were leaving in our car when we spotted a suspicious car (one that we had been watching for some time) and stopped to investigate. Upon questioning the woman and taking the dozen jumbo eggs from her hand, we found under the box of eggs, on her palm, $10. She wanted the eggs AND the money someone else had left! Another woman would come and stay in the stand room for so long, we wondered what she was doing. Finally we checked and found she was switching eggs from many boxes to make up what I guess she thought was the perfect dozen.

When we had "pick your own strawberries," as we did for many years, young children would come out of the field with their mouths all red, and I would ask them if they had any to eat, and they would look up at me and say, "No." Now that is innocence, and it is cute and understandable. When adults do the things they do, it is not acceptable, for they know better. This brings to mind a funny story about "pick your own strawberries." Each day of the PYO season I would take customers to the berry fields and show them where to pick and how to pick the berries. This particular day I took a man to the fields and he said, "Are those the berries down there?" I said, "Yes," and began to show him what to do. He turned around and walked out to the field and went to the farm stand and bought some already picked strawberries. Now his wife had each day stopped on her way home from playing golf and picked fresh berries for him from the fields. This day she had asked him to do her a favor and pick some berries for her. I must mention he was a tall man, but I still found it so funny that he had no concept of where and how strawberries grew. Apparently it was beneath him to pick them.

Over the years we have had our share of kleptomaniacs, and it never ceases to amaze us what things people will risk taking even when they may be caught. It embarrasses us and our employees more than anything to have to confront these sick people. It is difficult for us to understand that affliction, but we have to deal with it regularly. We have never prosecuted anyone in 37 years of business, although I wish we could have prosecuted a few of them. It is a shame some people spoil things for others, but that is the way with many things in life.

> "He that prigs what isn't his'n,
> When he's cotched 'll go to prison."
> "Happy" Webb

Archie at pumkin harvest time—1998

Helen at corn picking time—1998

CHAPTER TEN

FARM HANDS AND CUSTOMERS' HANDS

"There are different kinds of gifts, but the same Spirit.
There are different kinds of service, but the same Lord.
There are different kinds of working, but the same God works all of them in men."

I Corinthians 12:4-7

I have always been conscious of peoples hands, but mostly of Archie's. Anyone meeting him will notice his hands and that they are the hands of a hard worker, for they are rough, cracked, cut, callused, and his nails are broken, split, and almost always dirty or stained. But to me they speak volumes about him. One day he came into the kitchen with a kernel of corn that he had planted earlier on and showed me how it had sprouted. It had a single, white, two inch-long root coming out of the bottom of it and three slender, green leaves growing out of the top. I got my camera and took a picture of his hand holding the sprouted kernel of corn and eventually had it framed. It is one of my favorite photographs and now hangs above my desk—a poignant reminder of Archie and his love of farming.

This story brings to mind that there are many kinds of hands, both physically and figuratively. They speak loudly about who we are. Our hands are the servants of our minds. Our hands execute from our brains. Our hands may be young—smooth and soft, or callused—rough and worn, or old—wrinkled and blue-veined. Hands come in many colors, sizes, and shapes. If someone is an "old hand at it"—he is an expert. Our hands may be "full," meaning we are busy; on the other hand, if you are a "handful" you are difficult to handle. If we have "clean hands," we are not guilty, but if we have "blood on our hands" we are guilty. We can be helpful and "lend a hand." We can own something that is "secondhand," meaning it is used. We can "rule with an iron hand" denoting we are demanding and strict. We can "join hands"—show united support; we can "extend a hand"—offer a welcome; "give a hand"—help out or applaud; "wash our hands of it"—get rid of something.

Our hands may be "open" to prayer or to another person. Hands can labor, love, serve, and save. A child's hands can hold yours and thrill you with loving thoughts. A hand gently laid can give you comfort and reassurance.

Look at your hands. What do you see? What do they tell about you?

Helen Coll

To run a successful farm operation we need good workers or another term is "farm hands" and "many hands make light work," or as the case is, many hands get the job done quicker and easier. When we started our farm our first worker was a man who rented the apartment over our house. He lost his job and could not pay the rent, so he helped Archie put a concrete floor in a wing of our old barn, where we kept two cows; one was Suzanne's Holstein and the other was Mark's Guernsey. When this man had worked off his overdue rent, he moved out, but we were grateful he "paid" his rent and didn't just leave us with his debt.

For a few years Archie and I did all the farm work ourselves. He still worked for his father and we had the chickens in our old barn. We then expanded to his father's farm and we needed a worker to help us. We hired a young man, Albert, only for the summer and he was to live with us. Well he lasted one week. He was from the city (a neighborhood of Boston) and I think his family thought he should have the experience of working on a farm. But he had other ideas. Albert was off playing with our children and riding their bikes instead of working. One day he fell off a bike and broke his arm, this after working only a few days. He wasn't able to do too much with one arm, I still can see him trying to hoe with only one arm and not succeeding very well, so his parents came on the next weekend to take him home. He was just too immature to work a job.

"Let your prayers for a good crop be short—and your hoeing be long"
                    An Albanian saying

After Albert left we advertised in an agricultural publication and an older man applied. We hired him on his experience, sight unseen. We picked him up at the bus stop and brought him home. I introduced him to our family and when he saw Dave, who was probably two or three, he got down on his knees, in front of the chair Dave was sitting in and gave him a penny and started reciting his prayer, "Now I lay me down to sleep..." Well, I knew then and there that something was wrong with this picture, and we eventually found out what it was. First we got Waldo a nice apartment and set him up as to housekeeping needs; he came with one, old suitcase. We transported him to and from work on the farm. I decided this time that whoever the worker might be he would not be living with us. On several occasions we even drove him to visit his mother, who lived an hour away from us, and waited while he visited, then drove him back to Jaffrey. I was uneasy with him and his behavior but still didn't know why until one day he was so drunk he could not work. Earlier I had taken him shopping. It was a Sunday (back then you could not buy alcohol on Sundays), and he bought several large bottles of vanilla extract. When I told Archie about his purchase I asked him, "What on earth could he do with that much vanilla," he laughed and said, "Look in your cupboard at your bottle of vanilla and tell me what percent is alcohol?" Well it was 35 percent alcohol! Now I understood the purchase and his problem. We worked with Waldo for more than two years with a great deal of patience and kindness, but eventually he became so incapable of working we had to let him go.

Because our farm operation is so diversified we need workers in very distinct areas: working with the chickens (picking eggs and feeding), working in the egg processing plant (grading and packing), working in the farm stand (stocking and cashiering), and doing field work (planting, cultivating, and picking), and driving tractors and delivery trucks. We have had many long-term workers. One man, Ed, has been with us for about 25 years. Many others have made it almost that long.

Through the years we have been hiring people, we have seen times of abundance of workers and times of scarcity of workers, actually three cycles throughout our 35 years of employment. When unemployment is low we have difficulty finding people to do the work, but the only consolation is that everyone hiring is in the same situation.

The farm stand workers, for the most part, are high school and college age people. We have had many children in the same family all work for us. A sister tells a younger brother and so forth. In one family, the Wheelers, five of the six children, worked here; in another family, the Duvals, all four siblings worked for us; and in many others three and two siblings worked or are working here. I think of the Houghtons, the Krakows, the Kemps, the Kenny Colls, the Perkins, and there are more I probably have failed to mention but are valued just as much. I have gotten to know some children so well that we still correspond many years after they left our employment. Almost all have been faithful employees and very few have caused any problems. I have laughed with them, cried with them, sung songs with them, and think of them as partly my own. It is so gratifying to be invited to graduations, weddings, and have them bring their babies and children for us to meet.

Each of our children worked for us, for pay, when they were old enough. Also each one left our employment to work elsewhere. We encouraged them to work for someone else and find out how it is out in the "workforce." It is not easy to have your children work for you or for them to have to have you as employer as well as parent. It is difficult to balance both roles; parent/employer or child/employee. Peggy once told me I would regularly tell her she was fired, for this or that, but she kept on working until she was 16 and left to go to the veterinarian's office. All of our children are very good workers. They learned well how to be responsible, wage-earning adults. We are extremely proud of each of them. Suzanne worked at the local A&P store then started her own natural food store and now has a gift basket business and a wholesale fruit and produce business with her husband, Ray. Mark worked at a local garage and then started his own autobody painting business, which he ran for five years before coming back to the farm to work with us. Now he and his wife, Lori, are taking over the farm as we approach retirement age. Peggy worked in a local bank, for a veterinarian, and then operated, as she still does, her Cuts, Etc. business from her home. Her husband, Paul, works with us on the farm. Dave left to work at a local garage, came back to work on the farm, left again to start his own logging and trucking business and now works at a Mack truck dealership along with his wife, Kelly, and his in-laws.

One young woman was named Jodie. Jodie was a very special young woman; bright, intelligent, inquisitive, and just full of enthusiasm and life. We knew her and her family from our church and had watched her grow into a teenager. She applied for work in the farm stand and we gladly hired her. Archie gave her a nickname (something he does to those he likes). He called her Geraldine or Gerry for short. Jodie called us Mr. C and Mrs. C. Jodie liked to wear bib overalls and she enjoyed every chance she could get to work in the gardens. I remember her planting many, many lettuces one year. She also made banana bread to sell in the stand. I had a special relationship with her as we both liked to bake, sew and sing. When we set up the stand in the morning before opening for business, she and I would sing different songs. A favorite of both of us was, "Morning Has Broken," only I could never remember all the words. One day she gave me a pretty card inside which she had printed with a great deal of care three verses of "Morning Has Broken." I still have the card, a beautiful memory of our friendship for which I am very grateful. We watched her grow up, attended her National Grange achievement night, her wedding, and oh so sadly, her funeral. She died so very young of cancer. She had learned sign language and would sign songs. We saw her sign, "From A Distance" in our church on a Sunday and she died the following Thursday. She was one of the most beautiful people we ever knew, for she had inner beauty and serenity as well as outer beauty. We continue to be affected by her every day in many ways. We now know we were truly "touched by an angel," and she is still missed and dearly loved.

Throughout the years we have been very fortunate not to have had any bad employee accidents. The times we have had to call an ambulance were for a young man having seizures and for an older man having heart trouble. We have had cuts requiring stitches but really no big emergencies. Safety in the workplace, especially on a farm, is a big issue and requires the attention of all parties.

When our church assisted Cambodian refugees to resettle in our town, I offered to help the mother of one family learn some English. I had the pleasure of visiting their apartment regularly and bringing them gifts and learning about their customs. They liked to eat leftover cold rice with raisins as a treat; it made me think of rice pudding. They still come to our stand to shop all these years later. They are wonderful people who wanted their six children to become educated and independently established. The sister of the woman I taught, came later to the United States with her three children, and she worked for us for several years. She is a shy woman who liked to sing while she worked. I remember Iang wrapping her hair in her shirt, so it wouldn't get dusty while she picked eggs. We had the pleasure of watching her children grow up, marry, and have children of their own. One daughter worked in the stand and we attended her wedding, which was very interesting. She wore not one but two beautiful dresses during the reception and the food was delicious, although very spicy hot, and they served refreshing lylichee (a fruit) and unusual coconut soda.

When we had our first stand and the children were young, I had to watch them as well as take care of the customers. The children would be playing close by and our customers got to know them. One gentleman, Professor George, was a daily regular, and on this particular day, Mark had built a cage on his little red wagon and Peggy was in it pretending to be a monkey. When Prof. George saw them he quoted a humorous limerick about a monkey. The kids thought it funny and were impressed with his recitation. From that time on they called him the "monkey man."

Another customer was the "goat lady" for she had raised goats and had plenty of advice for us in raising our goat. Another was the "tomato lady," for she bought large bags of carefully selected tomatoes each trip here. I spoke to them by their real names, but the kids were young and knew them by nicknames.

Working behind a counter greeting the public every day can be pleasant and rewarding, but it also can be challenging and demanding. From the many business years I can recall three that were the most challenging and threatening. Two were males and they both were lawyers. Each talked fast, question followed question, always telling me what I should do and not do. Both my daughter-in-law, Lori, and I would comment, "Here he comes again," about each of them as a warning to be ready for the verbal barrage. Both lawyers happen to be from New York! One, I'll call Jim, was helpful and concerned to some extent, but the other, I'll call John, was not nice. John asked questions about our husbands and how they treated us, and why we were working so hard every day. John was demeaning, but I really think he thought he was being helpful and showing interest.

Another customer, I'll call Barb, demanded our complete attention and could "fire" questions at us steadily for the length of the time it took to wait on her. Barb always wanted to know what we were preparing for our husbands for supper, in detail with the recipes! She most often came just before closing and would keep us late. At first we felt she was interested in us, but then reality set in and we sensed it was all very superficial.

An extremely pleasing customer was Fleur. She is a photographer and artist who lived in Jaffrey for awhile and shopped with us. She was always pleasant, gentle, and quiet spoken. We felt respected by her. She gave me the use of her chockpot and recipe booklet to help me in planning and preparing meals, since I had to work late and then feed a hungry family. She took many, many photographs of the produce, inside and outside the farm stand, and then gave them to us. It was the first time I thought of the produce as art and it changed my perspective from then on. Fleur's life changed and she moved away, far away. She went to live on the Big Island, Hawaii. She remembered us with cards and letters until a time came when we were able to take vacations. Mark, Lori, and Paul (our son-in-law) were capable of taking good care of the farm business, and Fleur invited us to visit her in Hawaii. After several years of invitations we went to see her and her gorgeous island home. She graciously gave us her guest cottage to live in for two weeks and her car for exploring the island. She also took us on a four-day tour around the island. Such a marvelously generous gift! We are very grateful to her for her friendship and generous personality.

Many other customers' hands, too numerous to mention individually, have blessed us with gifts of every kind. We have been given paintings, photographs, food, farm memorabilia, books, articles, old tools, and milk bottles, and on and on. Dorothy created eclairs, Maria baked delicious apple pies (Archie's favorite), Dr. Jean made blood orange marmalade (my favorite), Edith brought us beet borsch, Barbara gave me a Rosemary bush and Charlie brings us all manner of food because he worries we don't take time to eat. During our battle against the location of a regional landfill on our farm land, we received help from numerous customers, from near and far, as well as Jaffrey residents. Another way customers have helped us to serve them.

In the fall of 1971 I was working our stand and our neighbor June came in. She said, "Here is something you might like," and she handed me a brown paper bag with a piece of rolled-up paper in it. When I removed the paper and unrolled it, there was a glorious watercolor painting of photographic quality of our farm in autumn, which was the view from her kitchen window, the same view I previously enjoyed when I lived there before marrying. She gave of herself, shyly and unassumingly. I loved it at first sight and had it beautifully matted and framed. It is a treasure to this day. June is an extraordinary artist and I had her do other oil paintings for me (two of our other farm, which is our view and one of Mount Monadnock) as well as a pen-and-ink drawing of our home.

I like to attend openings and enjoy exhibits at the Jaffrey Gilmore Foundation Civic Center in Jaffrey. A few years ago I attended a one-man show of our customer, neighbor and friend Fred Press, a renowned artist, and there was an oil painting of our home done in a winter scene. It was very beautiful and serene. I inquired as to the price and it was too expensive for me to buy. I told

Cultivating Life
A Story of Earth and Hearth

Fred I liked the painting very much. A few years passed and he sent us a card about another one-man show on Martha's Vineyard, and on the invitation card was a colored photograph of the oil painting of our home. I asked Fred for four more copies of the invitation, as I wanted to frame them for my children. He was very obliging. A few more years went by and we had become better friends. One day we were talking about the painting of our home, and I finally told him why I hadn't bought the painting. He responded, "Could you give me half of what I was asking for at the show?" I told him I would talk it over with Archie. Archie and I decided we could now afford to buy it. The next time I saw Fred in the stand, I told him we would like to buy the painting and he said, "It has been sold." I was devastated, couldn't speak, just went to the back room and told Archie it had been sold. He said, "Well that settles it. We can forget about it." I felt terrible that someone else now had the painting of our home, but what was done, was done. When Christmas came that year all our children and grandchildren were gathered at our home, as is our custom, for dinner and exchanging of gifts. After the opening of gifts had been completed, our children placed two chairs side by side and asked Archie and me to sit in them. They then brought in this large, gift wrapped box and placed it in front of both of us, and told us, "Open this. It is your Christmas, birthday, Mother's Day, Father's Day and any occasion for the entire year, gift!" Oh, such a huge surprise! There was the long-coveted painting and it was splendid! I cried, for I had not seen it since years earlier at the Civic Center and it is so beautiful. Now it was ours! What a special gift from our entire family and painted by our dear friend, Fred. It now graces a wall in our livingroom and always evokes favorable comments from visitors.

Other customers have given us paintings and others I have bought, both for our stand and our home. Local artists' whose works I have are: June Pratt, Ellie Gagnon, Gilbert Emery, Betty Boucher, Stella Bradford Scott, Mildred Turner, Grace Godwin Way, Lee Carter, and Jane Coffin. Photographers have gifted us with many gorgeous photos of various scenes around the farm: the view, the gazebo, the produce, our antique wagon, tractor, and implements. Each is appreciated and displayed. I think of Fleur Weymouth, Mr. Silvestre, Ray Haskell, and so many others too numerous to mention.

It is very satisfying to have customers appreciate us and our ability to farm and then demonstrate it by giving of their talents. It is very rewarding and gratifying to know we are helping and pleasing someone to the extent that they want to bestow favors on us. It touches our hearts to be appreciated and in turn makes our long hours of work worthwhile. These things money cannot buy, for when you give a gift you are giving a part of yourself. When someone gives you a gift, it goes beyond just a brief customer/clerk relationship. It speaks of gratitude, acceptance, recognition, reward. A gift can open up a relationship to become a friendship. A gift to us is another way to demonstrate thanks for the job we are doing. I have never felt any strings attached to any gifts, be they large or small, we have received over the years. Yes, some customers do try to take advantage of us, and yes, we do have shoplifters and thieves, and yes, employees do steal from us but, the percentage is much less and is by far outweighed by the good we see. To give something you have made or created is the most precious of gifts. Over the time we have been in business I knew people had given many treasures to us, but until writing this I never realized to what extent we have been gifted. We are very blessed in so many ways, and it is nice to actualize the extent to which we are appreciated. We have over the years fed many people, but they also have fed us with their love, concern, and tokens of fond appreciation for our life's work to give them fresh and healthy food. Early on, I am pleased to say, I knew our occupation was not just a job, for the people we work with and the people who buy from us and sell to us make it much more than just a job. It is a chance to be in their lives and have them in ours. That is not to say it is a totally wonderful experience, for one can grow tired of not having privacy, as with the lawyers and Barb, who wanted too much from us.

Women customers like to share recipes and men customers like to share information. Many times we are asked, in person or by phone, for information on chickens (growing, feeding, diseases, etc.), on crops (seeds, fertilizers, insecticides, herbicides), and on equipment (tractors, planters, trucks). Sometimes the requests are so long and in-depth we joke about charging for the "free" advice. After all, this is our business and our way of earning a living, just like a doctor or lawyer, but they do not give "free" advice. Sharing recipes, on the other hand, is a great free informational thing to do. When I finish this book I hope to write a cookbook on vegetables, fruits, eggs, maple syrup and chicken. I have a collection of cookbooks, as do many friends and customers, and I think our customers would appreciate a Coll's Farm cookbook.

Another "service" we have to provide from time to time is car repairs—from keys locked in the car, to dead batteries, to flat tires and more, Archie and Mark and Paul are called on to help out. These times of assistance are voluntary and complementary. On occasion they are rewarded with a thank-you note which is very nice to receive.

We also receive "free" advice from our customers like: where to vacation or where we can find particular items, about machinery needs, and old trucks available for sale. It is nice to have them interested in our lives and willing to share theirs. It is always surprising to find out how many remember our children and now grandchildren and tell us of "way back when" they came to our farm and now bring their families to visit.

Our eggs have drawn customers to us from the very beginning. Some first came when we had the "honor system" and they would help themselves and

Cultivating Life
A Story of Earth and Hearth

leave the money while they were vacationing in Jaffrey during summers. Now they make a trip from the city (Boston area) to buy eggs "from the farm." Also they will come in the fall to buy large quantities of vegetables and fruits to can or freeze. For many people freezing corn for winter's eating enjoyment is a necessity.

Every day we are gifted with smiles, pats on the shoulder, and kind understanding words; those alone are the greatest gifts. Over the last thirty-five years we have made many rich friendships, those that enrich our lives with their caring and the support of our family, and hopefully we enrich their lives with healthy foods and consideration and attention.

"Real gratitude, like joy, is a feeling, a spirit, an attitude that cannot be concealed. It has to be expressed."
Paul S. McElroy

"'Tis the gift to be simple, 'tis the gift to be free,
'Tis the gift to come down where we ought to be.
And when we find ourselves in the place just right,
'Twill be in the valley of love and delight."
A Traditional Shaker Hymn

Helen Coll

CHAPTER ELEVEN

EMINENT DOMAIN

"The right of a government to take private property for public use by virtue of the superior dominion of the sovereign power over all lands and jurisdiction."

Webster's Dictionary

Imagine, if you will, being invited to a meeting in your town and when you walk into the crowded room and finally find a seat there is a large map on an easel at the front of the room. As you look closer at the map you see your place is in the area which someone plans to take for the common use of all citizens. Well, that is exactly what happened to my husband and me in July 1988. I need to backtrack here and give you some information leading up to this situation so you may understand what we were up against.

In 1958 the State of New Hampshire took the only flat acreage on my parents' hillside farm and from the farm next door to ours, that of my future in-laws, for a new Route 202 highway from Jaffrey to Peterborough. That was the first time I heard of eminent domain (the right of government to buy land for public use, at what they think is a fair value), but not the last, I am sorry to say. From this first taking of land I learned what impact such a taking has on a family and a farm. I saw discouragement in my parents' eyes and heard it in their voices. This new highway was dividing part of our farm from the whole and cutting off the pasture land from the Contoocook River. Now quantity of water was always a problem for us on the dairy farm, and in summer it was at its worst. Except, that is, when the cows could be pastured on the front acreage, which didn't yield a lot of hay, and they could go down to drink from the river. With the new highway they no longer would be able to do that. My father protested and, as an act of concession, the state installed a very large culvert pipe under the highway for the cows to walk through to the river. It was a solution, but it would have been better if they had never taken the land in the first place. I have enjoyed showing my children and now my grandchildren where the "cow tunnel" is and walking through it, calling out so as to hear our voices echo, and straddling the water that sometimes is running through it.

Then in 1960 the Town of Jaffrey took 10 acres of land from our farm and 28 acres from my in-laws' farm for the purpose of locating a town sewer system and dump. This was the second eminent domain taking from us/our families and by far the most devastating. My father-in-law hired a lawyer on his behalf in hopes of gaining more money per acre for what they took (they offered $35.00/acre and he got $100.00/acre, five years and a court battle and lawyer fees later). I personally witnessed what it did to him. The case did not come to court for five years, and when it did it was not pleasant. I remember going daily to the Superior Court House in Keene for the trial proceedings. Many townspeople were testifying and lines of support were drawn and hurt feelings accumulated. I do not think he ever completely got over the battle. From it I learned to fear the words "eminent domain" and all they entail!

And so, in 1988 when we found ourselves faced with another taking of our farmland plus a new two-family house we owned, we felt sick to our very depths. This time not only did they want to take productive farmland and a house, but also surround our farm, home, and farm store with a forty-to fifty-five acre landfill for twenty-one towns and one city! It would mean the end of our business as we knew it, for it would present an enormous, potentially hazardous element bordering directly on our farm. We grow vegetables and strawberries and produce eggs, which we sell directly to the consumer in our farm store, and having in very close proximity a potentially dangerous in-ground hazard to our soil and water would be devastating. It would necessitate thirty to forty truckloads per day (130-150 tons/day) of garbage. Such magnitude was very difficult to comprehend and still is.

The evening of that first meeting was the beginning of the battle of our lives and the lives of our daughter Peggy and son-in-law Paul, our two sons Mark & Dave and daughters-in-law Lori & Kelly, my brother Ed Van Blarcom and sister-in-law Carmen and all the families and employees working on our farm (20+) and living on it or nearby. I immediately composed a letter to the editor, after a very sleepless night, stating five reasons we were opposed to the regional landfill taking our land.

My brother (Ed), who is a neighbor of ours and would be affected by this action, drew a large map (a close copy of the one from the meeting) showing the area involved, which we displayed at our farm store, along with a petition I wrote to the Selectmen of Jaffrey, requesting a formal meeting to present the facts to the townspeople of the far-reaching impact such a landfill would have on the health and economy of every citizen. At our store in one week we had 1198 signatures! We presented it to the selectmen, but they did not call a meeting. On several occasions I requested a copy of the map, but the district never provided us with one. They gave lame excuses, and the worst phone conversation of all the phone calls was the one in which I spoke to the chairman of the district. He was very demeaning and derogatory towards me. The district officials, the engineers, and the selectmen ignored us the best they could. We were an obstacle to their plan. They treated us as if we were invisible.

Helen Coll

The entire month of August, the busiest by far of our business year, we had to extend ourselves further to educate ourselves and our community on landfill use and misuse, safety, and impact. We had to learn about double-lined vs. single-lined landfills, gases building and being emitted, soil types, permeability, water aquifers and tables, drainage, seepage, waste to energy, traffic impact, road adequacy, bridge capabilities, and much more. We attended two and three meetings per week to learn about the Ashuelot Valley Refuse Disposal District, the Kimball-Chase engineering firm, and the personalities involved (for example, the treasurer of the district was the father of our town manager), everything concerned in choosing sites (we were at first one of seven, then one of five, and finally one of three) and what <u>rights</u> we have and how we could <u>avoid</u> being a site. During July and August my husband works about 120 hours per week and I work about 80 hours per week, and now we had to work longer and study and learn more than ever before. The potential of what we were facing was all-encompassing and concerned us directly and hundreds of other people indirectly. We had to fight and we had to win!

Many people came to our aid: family and friends attended both local and district meetings with us and gave strong moral help; citizens of the town supported us by signing petitions and writing letters, offering technical help or giving names and addresses of people they knew could help us; people from other towns also sited for the landfill offered advice and support (one gave me a crash course in soil types, permeability, drainage and seepage problems). I wrote letters to waste management councils, state legislators, United States senators, New Hampshire secretary of state, New Hampshire Commissioner of Agriculture, our representatives, engineering firms, conservation commission, solid waste committee, and more. My letter-writing skills and phone skills were greatly improved. I was not intimidated to call or write to anyone who might be of help. A forester came forward and told of the area around the landfill site being one of the best woodlots in the state that contained a Blue Heron rookery, one of the largest in the state with 18 active nests. Customers in our store offered suggestions and even more importantly stood tall and strong in our defense. They reassured us they were with us and wanted our farm to stay intact. They valued our farm and wanted to continue to buy our vegetables, fruits, and eggs. One customer secured an invitation for us to attend the Farm Aid concert by Willie Nelson in Keene and the chance to meet him and tell our story. We were not able to make it there because of the traffic jam that occurred that day, but we did receive favorable publicity.

By September we had thoroughly educated ourselves and the townspeople, and we realized the solution was for the town to withdraw from the district, for then the district could not locate in our town. The district representatives and town selectmen kept saying, "Wait and first see if they choose Jaffrey. Then make a decision." But if we did that, it would be over for us. At the very first district meeting we attended in Keene the chairman said they would first narrow down the sites and then use eminent domain to take the land. There it was again, for the third time in our life, EMINENT DOMAIN. It was not and is not FAIR. Furthermore, we are a 200-year-old farm, continuously farmed, which directly feeds thousands of people. Everything we grow (except for some of our eggs) we sell at our farm store—no middle man, no warehouse storage, no shipping—direct, field to home. To take productive farmland, that feeds people and contaminate it forever is not a wise or justifiable action.

The second petition was again to our selectmen requesting a special town meeting to consider withdrawing from the district. We only needed 12 signatures but were able to get 146 in one day. Through newspaper coverage, including the front page of the *Sunday Boston Globe*, and letters to the editor we were able to educate citizens as to what was transpiring, our concerns, health hazards, financial burdens (tax impact), traffic impact, river contamination, aquifer contamination, and the long-term problems of maintaining such a landfill after its 20-year life span. We paid for all advertising and printed up fliers to hand out and posters to display. A friend, Andy, made large buttons which we gave away, and another friend, Eunice, made T-shirts (both said "Don't Dump On Us").

From this time of battle we learned a great deal about trash and about political personalities! We listened to talks on trash to energy plants (problems of incineration and toxic ash), legislation to call for all plastic packaging to be either recyclable or biodegradable (our church initiated a policy to not use Styrofoam, and it is still in effect today; we use only paper goods), contamination of subterranean and surface water (rivers, aquifers, tributaries). We learned how to read maps concerning: soils, permeability, aquifers, drainage, and waste management technology for the future and the consequences (if we do and if we don't). Yes, trash is a huge problem, and we need to deal with it to protect our future, but the solution should not be worse than the problem, and taking productive farmland and contaminating it forever for a 20-year temporary answer is not a viable solution. We gained insight into people's personalities when under scrutiny and duress. For every person wanting to hurt us, we found 50 or more willing to help us. We were called NIMBYS (Not In My Back Yard), but I really do not feel we fit that name. It was not and is not a justified solution to provide a large district with only a 20-year trash solution by taking 200-year-old productive farmland directly feeding people! Our fight to avoid the taking of our farmland was 100% justified. Our townspeople did not need or want 30-40 trucks rolling through town every weekday with smelly loads of garbage on them, and the town did not need such a landfill contaminating an aquifer with the potential of supplying the town with pure drinking water, or contamination of the Contoocook River, or the loss of a farm store where its citizens can purchase fresh produce all year round. No, we were not NIMBYS, only hardworking, conscientious, and concerned citizens called on to fight for our livelihood and the greater benefit of Jaffrey citizens. What did the district offer the town? Reduced tipping fees (dumping fees) and a savings on mileage, for it would be located close by and save on transportation fees. Not enough, obviously.

On Saturday, October 15, 1988, a special town meeting was held: "to see if the Town of Jaffrey will vote to withdraw its membership from the Ashuelot Valley Refuse Disposal District also known as 53-b." My husband and I spoke to the issue, and after lengthy discussion the article was moved. The results were YES-266, NO-29. The article passed.

The newspaper articles said we were smiling and yes, I do suppose we were, but it was a bittersweet smile! That morning I had a sore throat and was feeling as though a cold was coming on. It became full blown the next day, and I was sick on and off for the next six months; I was physically, mentally, and emotionally drained. I felt fragmented throughout the battle time and I was continuously trying to be completely together once again. This did not happen until the special town meeting day when I started to feel whole again. I have said I would never go through that process again. Yes, the townspeople supported us, but the toll was almost too great. Now that 10 years have passed and I find myself opening up the entire issue for this book, I have an opportunity to look at it with distance. Would I do it again, if I had to? Yes, even though it was the most difficult and painful thing ever, I would have to do it for the greater cause: my family, our customers, and our town. A learning experience? Yes, but we would like to learn on our own, not out of such drastic and potentially devastating situations. This brings to mind a quote from Valorie Jackson that I read, "I've learned to pick my battles. I ask myself, 'Will this matter a year from now? A month? A week? A day?'" I think if something will matter more than a year from now, then fight for your rights and/or the rights of others so you will not have regrets in the future.

In 1990 The Town of Jaffrey had to close its present landfill (located close to us on land taken from us in 1960), and tests would be conducted on all the surrounding drinking water wells: three of ours, my daughter's, my brother's, and one other. The landfill itself had been surrounded with test wells for a few years, since 1976, and they knew that contamination was happening in some of those wells but never told us of it. The drinking water well at the duplex house we owned (the one the district wanted to take) was contaminated by some very serious industrial chemical solvents. This necessitated phone calls to the state DES (Dept. of Environmental Services) and the town's engineering firm to find out what these chemicals are, where they come from, how dangerous they are, and how we can get rid of them. We were scared and very worried, for two

Cultivating Life
A Story of Earth and Hearth

families, one being our son Dave, wife Kelly and infant grandson Benjamin who were living in the house and using the well.

The town was not moving very fast and was reluctant to take responsibility, and so this time we hired a lawyer to work on our behalf. This proved to be a waste of money, for we felt we knew more than he and he did not fight for our rights effectively. I think the only reason we hired him on this problem was that we were concerned about another battle with the town and this time did not want to go it alone. We were still in distress from the last "big battle." From this experience I learned that I am the most capable person to educate myself and negotiate on my behalf. In the meantime we purchased bottled water for all the families needs. Quickly this became very expensive and inconvenient, and winter was approaching. We decided to dig a ditch, below frost line, and lay pipe from our farm well, approximately 1000 feet, to the Dave's house to provide them with water. Finally the town was forced to provide us with potable water, which they did by installing a filtration system to aerate the water to rid it of the harmful chemicals. They must maintain the system, but we have to pay the electricity to run it. They continue to test the water at point of entry and after the filtration system yearly. This is still operating and will operate for years to come. They never did pay for the period of time, almost a year, we had to provide safe water for the families. They said we did not have their approval to do what we were forced to do. We felt the consequences were too great for the health of the families living in the house, and the DES and Public Health officials reinforced that with us in phone conversations and letters. Now we knew why they wanted to take that new house in 1988; I believe they already knew of the contamination problem. Now this happened with a single town landfill, so imagine if it had been a twenty-one town and one-city landfill that was leaking! We must always be very vigilant of our rights and well being. We must be wary of the town and state officials withholding information and yet be able to continue to negotiate with them for our security and safety. All this stems from the original eminent domain action in 1960.

Why don't people value the farmers that feed them three times a day?

CHAPTER TWELVE

THE DAY I RAN AWAY

It was Saturday of Labor Day weekend, September 1994, and I was in the garden picking many bouquets of zinnias, cosmos, snapdragons, asters, bachelor buttons, and salvias to sell in our farm store, when I suddenly had a completely overwhelming feeling of sickness and fell to the ground on my knees. A customer in the parking lot saw me and went to get my husband Archie. He came out with an employee and helped me to the house and to a chair. They then left me and returned to work. I expected Archie to come back to see how I was doing. There I was sitting in the chair feeling horrible and not understanding what was happening to me physically, when I heard a tractor running in the back field. I got up to see who was driving it and found it was Archie and there I was feeling so sick and deserted. I scribbled a note saying I was tired and needed to go away and threw some clothes in a bag (funny, I took only tops, no shorts). I got in my car and drove away, not knowing where I was going. I only knew I had to leave, to get away from this place that demanded more of me than I could give, and I felt no one was here to care about me. I drove and drove. Sometimes I had to stop because I could not see the road for the flood of tears. I can still hear my sobs of overwhelming sadness and utter despair, of my present situation and of my life. I felt out of control and my life was out of control. For now my answer was escape. As it was, I drove to the very end of Route 101, to the Atlantic Ocean at Hampton Beach. I parked the car and sat looking at the ocean with a very numb feeling; it was a pause in a long journey, a journey that was to take me from despair to a new self-realization. I had been to the bakery earlier in the day to pick up the bread order for the store and still had a loaf in the car. I ate some of it, pulling off chucks. I felt so alone, like there wasn't anyone in the world who cared about me and what was happening to me. I felt such isolation but in truth I had isolated myself.

I then continued to drive without any destination, just driving. My Aunt Evelyn had lived in that area and I found myself driving past her former home a couple of times. Several times I was lost; I didn't stop I just kept going. In all I drove around for 5 hours. I do not remember stopping for gas. I finally decided I would stay in a motel for the night. I had forgotten it was Labor Day weekend and when I stopped at a motel in Portsmouth they wanted too much money for a room. I asked the clerk about other motels in the area, and he said they were all full due to the holiday. He asked, "Why I don't you want the room?" I said "It's too expensive." He then asked, "How much can you spend?" I said "Sixty-five dollars." "Okay, you can have it for $65.00." I truly think he knew I needed the room, for I must have looked terrible, exhausted, lost and bewildered, and he took pity on me. As soon as I got in the room I undressed and lay on one of the beds. I was hungry, so ordered room service, the first time in my life, and ate exactly what I wanted, fruit cup and clam chowder, which seem so strange to me now. It was a large room with two beds, a table and chairs, worth more than $65.00. I sat in the middle of one bed and thought about calling Archie. It was late, about nine o'clock, and I thought I should let him know where I was. I called him. I remember my voice being a slow monotone and I cried a lot. I told him I was so very, very tired of everything. He pleaded with me to come home. I remember him saying over and over, "Just come home and we will talk about it, but just come home." He told me to get a good night's sleep, not to rush in the morning, take my time and drive home.

The next morning I slowly drove home and Archie decided to spend the rest of the day with me, an unusal thing for him that time of year. He wanted to shop for work shoes at the new Wal Mart in Rindge and insisted I go along, even though I said no because I felt so sick. In the store I kept looking for places to sit down, for I was exhausted. I was not the least bit interested in shopping; I only wanted to sleep. I don't remember if he found the shoes. We then went to a restaurant I had wanted to go to for some time, Lilly's on the Pond, but when there I could not enjoy it. I felt I would choke on the food and I just wanted to lie down. Monday, the holiday, I do not remember at all; I think I slept all day. Tuesday morning I asked our daughter Peggy to drive me to the doctor's. You see, I did not want to go to the emergency room on a holiday weekend, so waited until Tuesday and when I called him he said I had to see him in the emergency room anyway because he was on call there for the day.

I was there a total of four hours and had several EKGs done. Poor Peggy was waiting all this time with two year-old Isaac. Finally, Dr. Temple told me that my blood pressure, when I first came in, had been 250 over something (normally I am 90 over 60); I don't remember the figure. I was surprised but felt kind of numb. He told me I needed to change my lifestyle for it was having very detrimental effects on my health.

He was so kind and very thoughtful and considerate. He would come into the cubicle and talk with me and then leave, although I could see the ER room and what he was doing at the desk. I think he was giving me time to think about my situation and condition and taking time to prescribe what was best for me. He did prescribe some blood pressure medication and gave me the name of a therapist to call. He gave very careful consideration as to who would be the best therapist for me. He told me this therapist would be difficult to reach but that I should keep trying because he felt he was the correct one for me to work with.

Dr. Temple is a truly compassionate doctor. I have made several changes in my life, and will continue to change as I need to.

Farming is a wonderful way of life, if that life does not consume you! I truly believe God knocked me to my knees that day in the garden because I was not listening to my body and mind and adjusting my work life. Archie, honest and true, loves to work and loves his work. I, on the other hand, am a very hard worker but need breaks from it more than he does. It has been and I must say, continues to be, our biggest problem! He is able to work for six months without a day off; I can only do a couple of months. I desire more time off from work and I wish for him to want to be with me and hopefully find the same fulfillment in our relationship that he finds in his work. I feel I always have been by his side, working through the years, and now I need him by my side, enjoying some leisure and travel time.

I continued with the therapist for several months. It was difficult work, but out of the sessions, little by little, the answers and future plans manifested themselves. My desire to fulfill a longtime goal of obtaining a bachelor degree and taking time to write became apparent. Gradually I cut back on work time and finally enrolled in Leslie University and started writing this book. I graduated on November 20, 1998, one day short of my sixtieth birthday, with a Bachelor of Arts in Liberal Studies in my major, creative writing.

In 1995 I bought a cottage on Highland Lake in Washington, New Hampshire, about 35 miles from our farm. I now have a place to retreat to when I need to remove myself from the physical surroundings that still close in around me. I continue to take pleasure in my times there, and also my grandchildren and friends like to come for overnights. I am not able to go there often, but each brief stay is refreshing, relaxing, and rejuvenating. I enjoy kayaking on the beautiful lake and communing with nature. The water birds and wildlife are such a pleasure to me. The stillness and quietness of the hours spent there are truly a blessing, and I do not take them lightly but recieve them with full gratitude and satisfaction.

I still find myself crying tears for Archie's attention, although now less often. In words from *The Notebook* by Nicholas Sparks: "I love you for many things...love and poetry, and fatherhood and friendship and beauty and nature" "...You have taught me and inspired me, and supported me" (206). "In times of grief and sorrow I will hold you and rock you and take your grief and make it my own. When you cry, I cry, and when you hurt, I hurt. And together we will try to hold back the flood of tears and despair and make it through the potholed streets of life" (171). He speaks the very sentiments I feel deep within my heart and soul.

Cultivating Life
A Story of Earth and Hearth

CHAPTER THIRTEEN

FAMILY AND HOME

"My joy burns brighter when I tend to the glowing hearth fires of home."

Thomas Kincade

Creating a warm, comfortable, and happy home was something I now realize I was always preparing for and destined to do. I find it a very worthy and rewarding vocation. I have always felt and still do, that a farm is the best place to raise a family. Although I realize most people cannot do this, for us it is the answer. Every life lesson can be taught living on a farm and can be learned indepth and with actual experience.

In my earlier years, I learned from my mother and grandmother many skills I would carry throughout my life: cooking and baking, canning and preserving, sewing and quilting, interior decorating and good grooming. I was educated very early in life as to the need to be economical and self-reliant—plan ahead, be self-sufficient and most importantly, always "do unto to others, as you would have them do to you."

In our back yard in New Jersey was a large, tart, red cherry tree. When the cherries were ripe it was a challenge to get them before the birds did. We would pick them and then it was my job to turn the crank of the cherry pitter, which removed the pits and shot them out one shute and the cherries out the other. Then my mother would can them for winter pie making. Nothing can beat a tart, red cherry pie, especially on Washington's birthday in February. I think I can still taste those wonderful cherry pies with the pretty lattice crust and the red cherry juice bubbling through the holes!

Blueberries were in great supply in July in New Jersey, and all the family had to go blueberry picking for a Sunday's activity. I did not enjoy this because I was too fearful of snakes. We would go for a fairly long ride, and when we finally drove under a railroad bridge that said Susquehanna Railroad, I knew we were close to the blueberry fields where we would spend the day picking berries. I had to wear a belt with a large, metal can (like a coffee can) fastened on it, to pick into. I only remember seeing one snake in all those times. It was lying along a branch as I went to pick. Boy, did I scream!

Each summer my father would go berrying with some men friends for a day's picking in the swamps, where they had to wear rubber hip boots to protect themselves from the water snakes. I'm sure glad I didn't have to go there. My mother canned many quarts of berries for our delicious winter pies, tasty muffins, and sweet, steamy dumplings. Another item my mother canned was our own grape juice from the arbor by our back stoop. They were Concord grapes, very sweet and full of flavor. Mommy would can them with sugar and they had to age for several months, then we made a punch with the grape juice and ginger ale. We never had soda when I was growing up—only the grape punch. It was sooo good!

Both my mother and grandmother sewed. They made their clothes and mine and taught me to sew at an early age. By age eight I had made an apron, a slip, and a pair of pajamas, and they were made faultlessly. If I made mistakes, I had to take the garment apart and start over and do it correctly. This was taught with patience and kindness and thus I enjoyed sewing and still do. My mother was very willing to buy material for me to sew, whereas she was reticent to buy ready-made clothes. Most of my growing up years I had homemade clothing or secondhand. Mommy made some beautiful outfits for me and we had mother-daughter dresses for special occasions. The very first winter coat I had that was store bought was when I was in high school.

I told earlier of sewing with chicken grain sacks which made for very durable clothes and curtains. I still wish we could get them today for they were the best-wearing fabric. By the time I was thirteen, I was sewing dresses for my mother and for my grandmother. When I graduated from high school my gift from my parents was a sewing machine in a walnut cabinet. After our marriage and our children were born, I started making all their clothes. I would buy the fabric from the Sears Roebuck catalog, much of it in ten yard pieces, because it was cheaper for ten yards or more. One year I ordered ten yards of a red with white polka dot flannel for pajamas. Well, the order was lost and I called Sears about it and they sent out another order. In the meantime, the first order came soon followed by the second order. For years we all had red flannel pajamas, bathrobes, everything! A time came when I needed to help out with the family income and I decided I would start my own dressmaking business. I ran it from a room in our house for three to four years. I enjoyed it very much, but the kids were demanding of my attention and time. I had a room off the kitchen (the old summer kitchen) with its own entry door for my shop, and I could close the door to the kitchen and have privacy with customers, that is if the children cooperated. They liked to slide a ruler or yardstick under the door and wave it back and forth to get our attention, and sometimes would fight with each other. I became frustrated with the situation, and when I took the time to figure out if I was financially making gains, I found it was not paying me for my valuable time, so I terminated my dressmaking business. I missed it, especially doing weddings. When Suzanne was married in 1977, here on our front lawn, I made seven gowns for attendants, plus a long skirt with crewel embroidery on the front for myself. The skirt is now incorporated on the back of a wing back chair (formerly my mother's chair) in our dining room. When Peggy was married I made four gowns for her wedding. I had sewed for many women and some still tell me about things I made for them, which is gratifying. Just last month a woman who was visiting from Colorado Springs came up to me after church and asked if I remembered the black dress I had made for her. Imagine, this was before Dave was born in 1968, more than 33 years ago. I did weddings, tailoring, alterations, and dressmaking.

When my kids were active in 4H with the Chicken-of-Tomorrow contests, raising and showing sheep, making pottery, and exhibiting at Cheshire Fair, I taught 4H sewing to young girls for five years. It was a rewarding pursuit for me and I hope also for them. I continued to sew for my daughters until they could do it themselves. I remember one day before a dance Peggy came to me and told me she wanted to go to a dance the next night and wanted a long dress to wear to it. Not much notice! That evening I found a new, pretty green and white print sheet and some white lace and set about making her a long dress for the dance. It has always been a favorite picture of Peggy, taken by the lilac bushes in full bloom in her long green-and-white dress. Both of our daughters learned sewing and are very good seamstresses and can also do tailoring. I have tried some to teach our granddaughters to sew, but I really haven't made a strong effort, which is too bad for all of us. Times are different. Kids have a lot of activities and sports and their time is well taken up. Also they want to wear name brand clothing. It is unfortunate that they will not have the skill because not many people today wear homemade clothing, but it would help with sewing a hem or doing a repair.

Quilting is another ability my grandmother, mother, daughters, and I have. Grandma made more quilts in her lifetime than I can count. All were done completely by hand and mostly from used fabrics. To look at a quilt she made is always a trip down memory lane. I can pick out dresses of my great grandmother and all the way down to myself and clothes I had in early childhood. A favorite pattern of Grandma was the double wedding ring, and my mother's favorite was Dresden plate. I made a log cabin quilt for our bedroom and two quilts for the boys' bedroom. It is an in-depth project to make a quilt. First you must choose a pattern and the colors, then assemble the fabrics. Next you cut them out, then piece them together in blocks and sew the blocks together. You put batting (cotton or polyester fill) between the pieced-together blocks that are the top and the bottom fabric (usually muslin). Finally you have to mark a quilting pattern on the top and hand quilt the layers together. Grandma worked at her church in New Jersey with a group of women doing quilting for people who hired them for that purpose. They donated all the money to their church. Over the years they were able to buy many things for the church. They purchased furniture, redecorated Sunday school rooms, bought a furnace and air conditioning system, and even more that I am not aware of. It was a labor of love for them and they were very dedicated to their church and to doing the best job of quilting possible. They took great pride in their handwork and had a very social time doing the quilting. They brought a sandwich and drink for lunch and the hours flew by as they worked and talked the day away. They most often worked four days a week and took the summer off. I remember visiting them on a couple of occasions and I thought it was so nice my grandmother had this special gift to give to her church and at the same time enjoy a special sisterhood with the other women. She made me very proud of her and what she was able to do up into her eighties.

When Grandma was 89 she came to live with us. Dave was four and loved having her to play games with and to read and tell stories to him. Richard Scarry book *All About Working* was a favorite of his. He loved having Great Grandma read to him or just sit and look at the pictures and help him find the little glo bug hidden on each page. When Dave would bring the book to me, I would cringe a little, for he wanted to look at each and every page and would study them very carefully. If I skipped a page he noticed and pointed it out. I was either too tired or too busy for that large, involved book. But his great grandmother wasn't. They would sit together for long periods of time looking at each page. Grandma fell and broke her back in our house and never was able to walk again (I think she had osteoporosis), and she had to go to live in a nursing home because she required 24-hour-a-day care and I still had to work long hours. We all missed her but Dave did the most. We carefully selected a nursing home for her to live in, where she would have the most visiting time with family as possible, but my Uncle moved her back to New Jersey when he came home from Alaska. We visited her often at the two different nursing homes she lived at when she returned to New Jersey, her lifelong homeplace, but it was a question of traveling there with our big family. Rafael (I'll introduce you to him later in this chapter) was living with us during some of her stay and he enjoyed meeting Great Grandma. She lived to be 94. She was my mentor and champion and I miss her to this day. She taught me more than any other single person and she loved God and church and I am happy to say I also learned that from her.

Each summer for about three years Suzanne sent away to Rex Trailer (WBZ-TV personality) for a kit to help her put on a carnival to raise money for muscular dystrophy. The carnivals took place on our front lawn. She would plan the games and tricks and engage the help of Mark and Peggy to man the games and do the animal tricks. One game I remember was the "Penny Toss." Kids would toss pennies and try to get them to stay on a saucer greased with Vaseline, floating in a tub of water. Great Grandma, bless her, took on the job of cleaning the greased pennies, at the end of the day. This all took a great deal of organization: making posters and tickets, assembling and making the games, setting them up, and sending out invitations to cousins and friends. It took weeks to plan but was a wonderful summer activity, and they raised money for a very good cause. We felt it was good for the children to give of their time and talents to those less fortunate.

The children also liked to put on plays and shows. Suzanne wrote the plays and made up costumes, again enlisting the help of Mark and Peggy. They would "raid" my pantry for raisins, nuts, chocolate chips, Kool Aid, paper cups and muffin papers. These they would assemble to sell to Archie and me and both sets of grandparents. At one time Suzanne had a View Master slide viewer and a projector. She would show the slides and narrate them and Mark and Peggy would sell the tickets and refreshments. All proceeds were then divided equally among the three of them.

In my mother's and grandmother's kitchens I learned many skills, among them were preserving food for winter use. Late summer and early fall found them canning all types of vegetables and fruits. These were all carefully stored in the cellar and brought up on a daily basis for our meals. That was a job I had: to go down to the cellar and bring up to my mother whatever she needed to make for our evening meal. I did not like to do it for I found our cellar scary. It was a typical old cellar with dark corners, cold, damp stone walls, musty smells, coal bin in the corner, giant furnace in the center, and rickety, squeaky stairs. But, it held a treasure chest of good things to eat! We never had a salad, except in summertime. The rest of the year we ate canned vegetables and relishes and pickles.

When Archie and I married I "took up" canning. Each summer I would "put up" hundreds of jars of fruits, vegetables, pickles, jams, and jellies. One year Archie and I made root beer. We had a large closet where we stored the canned goods and we put the root beer in there too. Apparently some of the bottles were not sealed correctly and they spouted sticky, messy root beer all over everything. What a horrible mess! We also purchased a large freezer for storing our homegrown meats, which was soon followed by another freezer as our family grew. We have always eaten very healthy food and consider that one of the best "perks" of our lives on the farm.

Early in our marriage, a friend of mine came for a weekend stay. On Sunday morning June and I went to church, and when we got home Archie had made us a roast chicken dinner complete with apple pie. We were extremely impressed! While we were eating the pie Archie said, "That recipe you have for apple pie sure is a funny one. It called for Ritz crackers and never mentioned apples, but I put them in anyway." June and I laughed for the recipe was for a "mock" apple pie—no apples needed. But his recipe was even more delicious!

In the fall one year, when I was a novice at baking, I decided to surprise Archie with a homemade, from "scratch" pumpkin pie. I peeled the pumpkin (one we grew) and cut it into pieces (a difficult job) and cooked it. Then I mashed the cooked pumpkin and added the rest of ingredients and baked the pie. Well, it was the worst pumpkin pie! Full of lumps and bumps, I didn't know you are suppose to stain or puree the pulp. It was so much work I never made another one from "scratch" again.

A favorite family Sunday night happening was when Archie made donuts with the help of the children. They would all mix and measure and roll and cut. Archie did the frying in the hot fat. Then we would call up his parents to come and eat donuts for supper with us. They were so good—fresh and hot—but leftover ones were too hard. Clean up was my detail—flour everywhere—but it was so worth the effort for the wonderful time we all enjoyed.

We would also make Christmas cookies together each year when the kids were young. A favorite cookie of Peggy's that she made were called "Poodles." They were made of chocolate, butter, sugar, peanut butter, and quick oats. No baking—just drop by spoonfuls onto waxed paper. Peggy would roll out six feet of waxed paper all along the eating counter and spoon out the Poodles. They were more candy than cookie and everyone loved them. Dave's favorites were snowballs (actually called Russian Teacakes). They were made of butter, confectioners' sugar, flour, salt and finely chopped walnuts. He liked to roll the dough into balls. After baking them he rolled them in confectioners' sugar while warm and again when cooled. Um, um, good! They are also Archie's favorite cookie.

The children were able to learn many skills on a daily basis while working with Archie and me. When they were very young Archie did "custom haying" for some local people. I was the driver of the truck the hay bales were loaded onto and the children had to ride with me. That was never a favorite job of mine. It was always too hot, too sweaty, too-long hours, and the children wanted out of the truck. After a few years Archie felt it was not a good money-making proposition and he stopped doing it. Working with us the children developed good work ethics, strong morals, and lifelong values. Many hours they spent doing chores, which taught them responsibility, caring, perseverance. Suzanne and Mark helped me with canning and have done it for their own families. The conversations during canning time are priceless. I learned from my mother and grandmother, and my children learned from me. Everything was discussed at the kitchen table during those days of preserving food for winter. On school vacations each child had one day to plan, shop for, and make supper for that day. They could have anything they wanted to make but it needed to be a "balanced" meal. Each one had favorites they liked to make and to eat. My canning days came to an end when I was working such long hours at the stand and I had to do the canning at night. I would be in tears from exhaustion. I remember Archie telling me, "I'll buy you a case of canned tomatoes, but just don't knock yourself out over canning them yourself. Its just not worth it" He didn't like to see me so upset, tired, and frustrated and felt they weren't worth the time and effort. It took me a long time to get over not doing canning, especially our own tomatoes and peaches, for nothing tastes as good as homegrown. But I had to weigh the options and I decided my efforts had to go into the business. It was a sad conclusion for me but a necessary one. It has been many years since my last canning endeavor and now I choose not to do it, even though I have more time. Such is life, same as with the dressmaking—we all have choices to make.

"Bless this house as we come and go. Bless this home as the children grow. Bless our families when they gather in. Bless this house with love and friends."

Anonymous

When Suzanne was in her junior year and taking Spanish classes, she came home from school one day and told us she would like to be an exchange student, and had chosen to go to El Salvador. We explored this idea together and with the school and felt it was a good opportunity, even though we were apprehensive about her going to that particular country due to beginnings of their political unrest. If you sign up for the foreign exchange program, you must be willing to be a host family and take a student from another country and culture into your home. This was an easy decision for us, for we have always enjoyed meeting people and showing them hospitality. It was decided we would take a student for Suzanne's senior year of high school and the paperwork was completed. Suzanne, on the other hand, decided not to go into the program.

And so in June of 1976 we were informed a young man (15) from Mexico was coming to live with us for the school year (Sept.-July). In July we received a phone call from a man speaking Spanish (we do not speak or understand Spanish), that in essence told us that he and his wife were coming to our farm to visit us, and that they were the parents of Rafael, the student arriving in Sept. They called from Logan Airport in Boston, had rented a car and were driving to New Hampshire that very day! They arrived just in time to enjoy lunch with us on our back porch. Conversation was difficult but they were very pleasant and then they took a quick tour of the farm stand, met Archie, Mark, and Dave (Suzanne and Peggy were away). As fast as they came, they left. Later we realized they just wanted to know where their son was going and who he would be living with.

On Sept. 7, Rafael arrived in Boston where we picked him up at Logan Airport. He was a handsome young man and I loved him from the start. The ride home was strained, as Rafael spoke minimal English. Peggy and Dave went with us. Once at home we settled Rafael into Mark's room, which they would share for the year.

Gradually, very gradually, he learned English. He was a handsome, very pleasant, courteous young man. For a couple of months I was the one making the efforts to communicate with him. The kids seemed shy and insecure around him. I remember one day I was trying to communicate something to Rafael while he and the other kids sat at the eating counter we had at our kitchen island. One of them said, "Mom, he's not deaf, he just doesn't understand English!" It was my inclination to speak louder if he didn't understand what I was saying. After that I tried to keep my voice on a lower level but I remember still raising it if he didn't get the point of the conversation. Later on we were all able to laugh at my attempts to talk with Rafael, and he understood and forgave me for yelling. Another day we were out for a drive and stopped for ice cream cones. Apparently Rafael didn't want to finish his cone and just as we got to the Main Street of Jaffrey, he wound down the car window and was about to throw out his cone when I yelled, "Stop, don't throw that out!" He was very shocked so I then tried to gently explain about littering the road. Later I found out that in Mexico, if you don't want something, you just throw it down right where you are. Rafael's family values were different from ours. His family had maids and a gardener where they lived in Mexico City. When he first came I had to teach him to pick up after himself his towels and dirty clothes. At home he must not have had to do for himself at all. His father owned an industrial septic systems business. They traveled quite a lot to the United States. They had all been to Disney World in Florida. I thought they were rich compared with us, but he would say, "No! You rich. You have land and much money." It was a subject we would tease each other about.

Christmas that year was special having Rafael to celebrate it with us. We bought him the same presents we gave to our other four children. We totally accepted him as our son. Memories of him flood my mind: his love of cheeseburgers (he could eat three in a sitting) and pancakes (I never could fill him up with them), his use of musk cologne, and his desire to have hiking boots, which were all the rage with young people at that time.

His cousin, Hugo Cadaviego from Guadalajara, Mexico, was living with a family in Hudson, Massachusetts, as an exchange student. On several weekends and during school vacations we brought Hugo here for visits. It was good for Rafael and Hugo to have the chance to talk together and submerse themselves in their own culture for a short while.

Rafael did phone his family, but not often, and he was supposed to write to them, as were we, on a regular basis. I wrote to his mother, Maria Luisa, and she wrote to me, but it was a chore to get Rafael to write home. They sent him some money but did not send Christmas presents. He told me it is difficult and expensive to send gifts. I sent some to his family (father, mother, brother, sister) and told him that I had done this and he was upset. He said it would be a big inconvenience for his family to get them at the post office, and it was questionable they would ever get them. I never heard that they did receive them.

When Rafael came he brought gifts to each of us. Suzanne, Peggy, and I received gorgeous, long, wool, sweater coats with beautiful designs hand-knitted into them. Suzanne especially loved hers and wore it a lot. Archie, Mark, and Dave received hand-woven shirts also with designs in them.

Throughout the year Rafael became a member of our family in every sense of the word. He was loved like a son and like a brother. He enjoyed going skiing and liked the snow. I would tease him about the weather, for I thought it was very hot where he lived. But he told me Mexico City is in the mountains and it is sometimes cold there. I did not believe him. Many years later Archie and I flew into Mexico City and I could see the mountains, but it was May then and very hot. While he stayed with us the movie "Saturday Night Fever" was popular and Rafael liked John Travolta. He listened to the music and liked to dress like Travolta. At Christmastime he would always sing "Feliz Navida" when he heard it on the car radio or at home. Rafael went to the prom with a date and I made him a corsage for him to give to her. He bought a three-piece, light green suit to wear to the prom and to wear going home. He looked very handsome in it with his dark hair. He also bought an expensive camera and perfume for his mother. The day came when he had to return to Mexico. It was a very poignant and tearful good-bye when we took him to Logan for his flight home.

After graduating from school in Mexico City he became a photographer and a flight attendant, but had aspirations of becoming a singer. His mother had developed breast cancer and the money just wasn't there for him to go onto college, so he took a flight attendant job and was able to get discount tickets for his Mom to go to Houston, Texas, for cancer treatments. That was the true heart of our beloved Rafael. We spoke on the phone from time to time and always on Christmas. We kept asking him to come back for a visit and in return he asked us to come to Mexico. When Mark and Lori were married in August 1983, they went to Acapulco, Mexico, for their honeymoon, and Rafael came and spent several days with them. They loved having him there. He bought them a marble chess board and set of figures as a wedding gift. Later Mark made a coffee table from a thick slab of wood and embedded the chess board in the center of it. It is a wonderful piece of furniture to remember Rafael by as well as their honeymoon. Rafael was very proud and did not want us to send him the money for a plane ticket. Finally, out of desperation to see him again, I sent him the money to fly here. Nine years had past since we had last seen him and we were so excited to have him coming. We knew approximately when he would arrive because he was first flying to Los Angeles as part of his job as flight attendant, and then would purchase a ticket and fly to Boston. One night around the time he was to come, we got a call from a woman in California who said she was a friend of the Mujica family. She told us Rafael's plane had crashed upon taking off from the airport in Mexico City into the side of a mountain, and all on board were killed. We were numb, totally in shock. How could this happen? Such a wonderful, talented, loving young man, gone forever from all who loved him so dearly. And why now, when we were finally going to be together again? We talked with his family and expressed our sincerest condolences, but still it did not seem possible he was gone and we would never see him again. While Rafael lived with us we were responsible to see he attended church. We had asked the Hampsey family, who are friends and attend the Catholic church, if they would take Rafael to Mass each week, and they did this faithfully for the entire time of his stay with us. After his return home, Kevin Hampsey visited Rafael in Mexico City. When Kevin came back he brought me a beautiful sapphire and zircon ring, a gift from Rafael. Several months after Rafael was killed, the Hampseys' had a Mass said for Rafael on Ascension Day, May 7, 1986, and we attended. Finally there was some closure for us.

Rafael's lovely mother died, after a long battle with breast cancer, a couple of years after Rafael died. His poor father, brother and sister had suffered tremendous losses. This wonderful family we had come to know and love so well, was experiencing their darkest hours and we were so moved by their pain and sorrow. I had Maria Luisa's beautiful letters to remember her by, the ones she had written to me while Rafael lived with us and through the years after he went home, but they were in Spanish. A friend, Randy Cournoyer, asked another Mexican exchange student, Gabrielle, who lived with the Cournoyer family, to translate them for me. They are a wonderful memorial to Rafael and Maria Luisa Mujica.

In 1990 a phone call came from a family in Tapachula, Mexico. It was from Ileana Wong, a cousin of Rafael's, and she wanted to come and live with us for the last half of the school year. We were very excited to have her come. Again we found ourselves at Logan Airport to meet a member of our extended Mexican family. Archie and I were carrying a sign for Ileana, excitement and apprehension rising, and we finally saw her beautiful face and smile. It was very emotional for all of us, meeting Ileana, thinking of Rafael. She brought many gifts for our family and a special silver tray from the Mujica family, carefully carried on the plane with her. We also fell in love with Ileana from the first moment, as did our then five grandchildren. Archie and I did not have any children living at home by then, so we were able to devote a lot of time to Ileana. We took her on a trip to Montreal, Canada, in May, and had a marvelous time showing her the sights. She was so excited to see the city. We have many pictures of our adventures at the underground city, in a horse-drawn carriage, at the botanical gardens and the former Olympic sights. In June she went to New York City with a group girls from school. She loved New York City. Where she lived in Tapachula, Chiapas, Mexico, only six miles from the Guatemala border, was more country than where Rafael had lived in Mexico City. Her father owned a coffee plantation and raised beef cattle. Earlier I told about the corn soup we had at her lovely wedding. That was the first (and only time) we have been to Mexico. Ileana returned home in June 1990 to attend college. She went to the University of Monterrey, in Monterrey, Mexico. She did very well in the international commerce studies but became sick for part of her junior year and so requested to come and study at an international school in Cambridge, Massachusetts, to make up courses she had missed. We were elated as we would get to see her again, and this time we met her mother and sister. That year we had Ileana and two of her roommates from Cambridge come for Thanksgiving weekend with our family. They all enjoyed helping with the meal preparations, although in Mexico they had servants do this for them. In May 1997 Ileana was married in Tapachula and Archie and I went to the wedding and met Ileana's family, met Rafael's father, brother, sister, and their families, and we saw Hugo and his family again. It was the most marvelous sensation and our first vacation in Mexico. I realize now that the experience of being a host family for an exchange student was an extraordinary happening, and it only piqued my desire to know, understand, and love others' cultures. If I decide to get my master's degree it will be in intercultural studies.

Another story of a foreign student we came to know briefly, was Geraldo Ricoy, also from Mexico City. I received a phone call requesting we take a male student for a week or two until he could go to a host family in Contoocook, New Hampshire. Peggy, Dave, and I drove to downtown Jaffrey and were waiting on the bridge in our car for the arrival of this student. We were nervous and apprehensive, as you get before actually meeting someone you do not know. Finally a car pulled up and out came Geraldo. He was a very good looking young man and we all enjoyed his pleasant company for the two weeks and were sad to take him to another home for the remainder of his school year. This took place after Rafael had just left, and I think we thought no one could take Rafael's place, but we found ourselves surprised that Geraldo would have been very nice to have living with us after all.

> "If walls could talk, we've often thought, what stories they would tell. But if we're slow to grasp the message of an open front door, a clean-scrubbed floor, or a handmade object comfortable with its age and imperfections, perhaps we're just not listening well. The language of a house is visual. The soul of a house is memory. And it speaks to the heart."

Helen Coll

Anonymous

Our house was originally a wooden four rooms down and two up, Cape style home with a granite and stone cellar under it. Over the years it has seen many changes. We still have the cellar only under the front two rooms, with crawl space under the back rooms, and under the wing of the house it is drag space part way and the remainder is on a cement slab. We have always had it painted white with dark green shutters. The roof is a gabled style and supporting the porch across the front are Victorian-style posts. The wing of the present house was moved here from somewhere down in the front field many years ago, before anyone I know had lived here. The town historian, Alice E. E. Lehtinen, told me about it being moved here and connected with the main part of the house. She enjoyed many holidays here with the former owners, the Jurvas, although I think she had read about that information while writing the town histories. The windows are double hung, six over six panes of glass some of them are old, wavy, bubbly glass. It is simple in plan, a plain and functional farmhouse of modest means, not a wealthy Colonial farmer's home.

When we moved here in July 1961 it was in very poor condition. Our first night here Archie said he didn't like the place at all and thought we should move back to his parent's apartment. I said he could go but I was staying. We stayed. The house had a winter kitchen (the larger, with a sink and hole for a pump) and a summer kitchen (the smaller, no sink), and neither had any cupboards, counters, nor a single drawer, but each had a pantry. The summer kitchen eventually became my dressmaking shop. On my birthday that first year in the house, Archie gave me a large, black, rectangular tray with a white, a blue, and a pink hydrangea painted on it; all the colors of our bedroom. I hung it over our bed and it still hangs there through 40 years and many changes. I love it as much as the first time I saw it and I love the fact he had such good taste in choosing it for me.

It took us twelve years of working with very little money (because we didn't have any) to do over all the rooms. In the process we found many interesting items from the past. A hand wrought hammer (my favorite find, from inside a bedroom wall; someone must have left it there and built the wall around it), an adz (a tool used for trimming out or shaping), a broadhead ax, many other small tools and pieces of pottery, a hand-carved, large wooden spoon, an antique drill with wooden handle, some sleigh bells and many, many horseshoes. Also in the walls we found old corn cobs and many skeletons of various size animals. In outdoor areas where they dumped their waste, we have found bitters bottles, an inkwell, and other bottles as well as broken pieces of dishes in patterns of blue, brown, and pink. Each item we come across becomes a treasure of our farm's past and we place them in our kitchen, on the mantel, on the hearth, or hang them from the beam ceiling. They make us think about who made it, how they used it,

Cultivating Life
A Story of Earth and Hearth

and to which family and time it belonged. Each item or fragment is a gem to us and a remnant of a life lived here in another time—touchstones to the past.

The original three-room apartment upstairs soon became three bedrooms for our chidren for about twenty years. Then the children gradually left home and we no longer needed the bedrooms. Peggy was getting married and Archie suggested we make the upstairs into a three-room apartment once again. Peggy lived there for three years before moving into the new home she and Paul built. Then Mark and Lori moved in and stayed for six years until they built their new home. Today the apartment is rented out, as it was when we first moved here. The original woodshed on the house became our living room. Mark did the construction from my ideas. It is a beautiful oak contemporary room with large plant shelf and big windows. I have an antique, cranberry glass hanging lamp which is now electrified, from my great-grandparents home in New Jersey, the same home I lived in for 13 years, hanging in the living room. Mark also renovated our dining room. We kept that in the colonial style with wide pine board wainscoting, beam ceiling, fireplace with a Franklin front on it, and with gorgeous raised pine paneling over the mantel. Over our table hangs another beautiful antique lamp of my great-grandparents, which has also been electrified. Mark is very talented and I am blessed to have him share his abilities with me. He has helped us remodel our home to what I envisioned. The only room that has been added to our house is a new study for me to work from. It is a lovely, north-lighted room, painted white and relaxing green, with a wall of bookshelves, a window seat full of pillows, and a view of the opposite hill and the two farms, plus our back fields. I have an antique schoolmaster's desk I use for writing, a business desk, and a computer desk. I'm all set for work! I studied work areas of writers while at Lesley and then created my own and I love it.

This wonderful old farmhouse we have made into our very own haven against all life's storms, still stands full face to the south, well kept, loved, comfortable but by no means perfect. Down through the years it has heard the voices of many couples discussing farm life, making business decisions, heard the laughter and the cries of countless children as well as adults, seen babies born and people die, harbored baby animals and sick animals. It holds many secrets and memories of bygone days. It has been and continues to be the heart of this farm's life and the lives of the families who have lived here.

"Wherever there is a farm, there is the greatest opportunity for a true home."

Calvin Coolidge

Helen Coll

Rafael Mujica—1976

Ileana Wong—1990

CHAPTER FOURTEEN

AND NOW...THE REST OF THE STORY
(a saying of Paul Harvey)

"It is a short word, but it contains all:
it means the body, the soul, the life, the entire being.
We feel it as we feel the warmth of the blood,
we breathe it as we breathe the air,
we carry it in ourselves as we carry our thoughts.
Nothing more exists for us.
It is not a word; it is an inexpressible state indicated by four letters."
Guy De Maupassant

"These three remain: faith, hope and love.
But the greatest of these is love."
1 Corinthians 13:13

Making a home, building a farm business, and raising a family has been our focus for 43 years, since Archie was 20 and I was 19. It has been a "wonderful life," as Jimmy Stewart said.

All of it has been rewarding, but having grandchildren to love and be loved by, is definitely "the frosting on the cake." They are the light, hope, and love of our lives, and give us faith in the future; and like most grandparents ours are the brightest, most intelligent, good-looking grandchildren one could have. We have lived as we chose and been very fulfilled, but knowing each of our children is happy and fulfilled in their lives is gratifying beyond anything we could have planned. Suzanne is an excellent business woman, destined to lead, creative, and is a thoughtful and kind person. Mark is devoted, inventive, and an abiding supporter, conservative and practical. Peggy is independently lighthearted, artfully ingenious, respectful, loving and caring, a great mom and friend. Dave is hardworking, courageous, personable, positive, and an inspiration and luminous example for others.

Suzanne Helen is now 42 and married to Raymond LeBlanc. Together they own and operate Amherst Fruit and Produce, a wholesale produce business, as well as Suzanna's Gift Baskets in Milford, New Hampshire, a half hour drive from us. Their son Ryan Matthew, 22, is manager of car audio installations at Tweeter in South Nashua. He has a dream of owning his own home by age 25 and is well on his way to that goal. Their son Reuben Paul, 19, works with them in their produce business and enjoys doing Disc Jockey work in his spare time. They are very handsome and personable young men who enjoy many friends and fun times together. While in high school they both played football, and Reuben also played lacrosse and wrestled. Suzanne and Ray have plans for retiring to Grafton, New Hampshire, in the near future. They will operate a small farm and maybe a Bed & Breakfast business once living there full time, as Suzanne loves to cook and decorate their large home. Ray is an outdoorsman, who likes to hunt and snowmobile and ride his motorcycle.

Mark Richard is 40 years old and he and his wife Lori are in the process of buying our business. It is a five-year purchase plan, and hopefully the business will generate the money for the purchase so they will not need a mortgage or loan. Archie and I still own the real estate property and will rent it to them for now. Their son Joshua Mark Richard, 11, is in the fourth grade. He is an enormous help to his Dad and Grandpa. He can drive anything and does so very well. This past fall I looked out the kitchen window and saw our one-ton dump truck dumping load after load of dirt, and who was driving the truck? Joshua! He handled it like a pro. He is a loving and concerned young boy. He has some wonderful compliments and comments for us, and always is very interested in the business and has his finger on the pulse of what is really going on. Mark is a loving and caring father and husband, a very capable manager, and has many good ideas about the future of the farm operation and, along with the help of Lori, we are sure they will materialize. Lori has worked here for 19 years, starting as a clerk in the farm stand, then to doing office work, to now being fully in charge of the office and helping Mark in any capacity he requires. They are a dedicated couple with vision for the future of this operation and raising their son on a farm and possibly securing his future as a farmer someday. This will be the first time in the history of this farm that it passed from one generation to another. We have lived here the longest of any family thus far: 40 years this summer, July 2001.

Peggy Anne, 39, is married to Paul Despres and they have three children. Peggy owns and operates her hair salon business, Cuts, Etc., out of a shop attached to their home. She chose that profession so as to be available to her children and be self-employed and bring income into the family. She has built up a good and faithful clientele. She is a very dedicated parent who sincerely enjoys her children and wants the very best for them. Their first child died in utero at nine months, and Peggy went through the delivery with Paul and me by her side. Shane Steven was born and he was a beautiful and perfect baby but not alive. It was exactly one week before Christmas. This was terrible blow to them and also to Archie and me. It was very difficult to see them so hurt, but they were so loving and supportive of each other it only made their marriage a very strong one. Eleven months later Lyndsey Ruth was born. She is now 15, a freshman in high school and learning to drive. She enjoys her friends, does well in school, and is an outgoing, happy and athletic young woman. She just earned her senior life-saving certification. Whitney Kate, 13 and in the seventh grade, is a very giving young woman. She is a delightful person who enjoys reading, singing, dancing, and having fun with her friends. This year she is on the Swat dance team of the Dance Institute program. Both girls attend Camp Takodah (a YMCA camp) each summer. Isaac Paul is eight and in the second grade and loves anything to do with science and playing out-of-doors. He is bright, happy, caring, sensitive and thoughtful of others. This year he is in the Cub Scouts, which he is enjoying. He helps his Dad work on the farm and loves to drive the small Kubota tractor, the one used for cultivating between the rows of vegetables. All three children are on a swim team and compete locally and statewide. Last year their team won first place in their division in New Hampshire. They have been swimming year-round for six years. It is a big commitment for their parents, but the benefits far outweigh any inconvenience. It is a healthy, competitive sport in which they can gain achievement as individuals as well as a team. Paul works with us on the farm. He does many of the deliveries of eggs into the Boston markets, runs the greenhouse operation and does much of the field work. He likes people and enjoys talking with customers in the farm stand as well as customers on our routes. He has worked here for eleven years, and sees his future here on the farm. He is a valuable asset to our business and possesses the many talents and abilities it requires to be successful in this type of enterprise.

David Lewis is now 33 years old and has been married to Kelly for eleven years. They have two children: Benjamin David, 10, and Emily Elizabeth, 8. Ben is a delightful young boy who takes pride in helping his Dad and Mom. He is a good student at a Christian school that both children attend along with their cousin Joshua. Ben loves to ride his four-wheel ATV (all terrain vehicle) in summer and his snowmobile in the winter. He enjoys the out-of-doors and caring for his four cows. Emily is a happy, carefree young girl who likes to be in constant motion, be it jumping rope, roller blading, or anything to be active and moving. She likes singing to her CDs with her microphone. She is an excellent student and enjoys school. They are both very loving and giving children. Kelly is office manager and vice president of Stateline Mack Trucks, which is owned by her parents. Dave is working there as general manager. They also own a firewood business. For many years Dave owned a logging business, but on a most unfortunate day, June 3, 1999, he had an accident which changed his life.

It was a nice sunny day and I was in the house. A little after noontime I was not able to concentrate on what I was doing so I went into my office, where I looked out of the window at Dave's house across the hill, and thought, "I wonder how they (Dave and family) are? I haven't seen or talked with any of them for a few days." I then felt a wave of uneasiness. I sat down on the windowseat and had an urge to talk with God. It came to my mind that Archie was at the doctor's office for a routine physical and I sensed something was wrong with him and so I said a prayer for him. Now this is a very unusual thing for me, to stop in the middle of the day, feel uneasy, and take time for a prayer. The phone rang and it was Archie. My heartbeat raced. He said, "I just heard Dave has had an accident but I don't know where." I hung up the phone and called the local hospital to inquire if David Coll was there. They said no, he wasn't, and they did not have any communication that he was coming in. I put the phone down again and it rang as soon as the handle hit the cradle. It was Archie and he said, "Come down to the stand with the car. We need to go to Mt. Wachusett." My mind was saying, "Mt. Wachusett? Mt. Wachusett? Why there?" Kelly had called from work and told Archie that Dave was hurt and we needed to go to Mt. Wachusett College in Gardner, Massachusetts, as Dave was being taken there by ambulance to be airlifted to a hospital. I picked up Archie and I drove; mouth dry, heart beating fast, and with very little conversation. We passed the scene, which was a wooded area, and the rescue workers were still there, and then to the college. Once there we jumped out of the car and ran to where we saw Dave on a stretcher next to a helicopter. I kissed him and told him I loved him. He looked at me and I thought he knew me. They loaded him into the helicopter and off it flew. A worker gave us printed directions to the University of Massachusetts Medical Center in Worcester, Massachusetts. We took Kelly, who had arrived in her vehicle from work, and Archie did a careful job of driving us safely to Worcester. We had to stop for bottles of water to drink as our mouths were so dry. Kelly and I sat in the back seat, holding each other and praying for Dave.

When we arrived at the hospital we were escorted to a private waiting room in the emergency department. I then knew for sure this was very serious.

Dave had been working that day cutting trees on a woodlot, and his two workers were also there but in other areas of the woods. They do not work side by side, but stay a distance away from each other, so as not to be of danger to one another. Apparently Dave was cutting a tree and another tree must have been "hung up" as they say, and he did not know there was a "hung up" tree nearby because it hadn't been marked. Usually you mark a tree when it is cut and it does not fall so that it will not fall as a surprise later on when disturbed. The day turned dark and the wind began to blow and this tree, a large maple, fell, hitting Dave's hard hat (miracle number 1, it saved him from brain damage) on the back, right side, knocking him face down on the ground, breaking his right shoulder blade, all his ribs on the right side, and his backbone at chest level. How long he lay there for we do not know. One worker drove by where Dave was working and didn't notice anything unusual, but when he came back through about a half

Cultivating Life
A Story of Earth and Hearth

hour later, everything was in the same place (saw, equipment) and he didn't see Dave anywhere. He stopped the motor and called for Dave. He heard a muffled sound and thought Dave was far off in the woods, but upon calling again and looking closer he saw Dave was pinned under a felled tree. He cut the tree and somehow got it off of Dave. Dave asked him to turn him over and give him a drink of water. Dave kept telling him, "Straighten my legs." He had a cell phone and called for help. The fire and rescue teams from Winchendon and Gardner came. They secured his head and body onto a rescue board so they could carry him the half mile out of the woods to the ambulance.

A helicopter was already in Gardner, Massachusetts (miracle number 2) to take a man with heart problems to the University of Massachusetts Medical Center, but instead they flew Dave directly there without any further delay. He arrived an hour or so before we did. When we got there they let us go into see Dave very briefly. The impact of seeing him there in the emergency room was startling and so very vivid. He was moaning in excruciating pain and his eyes were pleading with us to help him. He had black dirt from the forest floor all over his face and in his eyes, nose, ears, and hair. We each comforted him, told him we loved him and would be there for him, to allow the doctors and nurses help him.

We were then back in the private room waiting for a doctor to come in and speak with us. A hospital spokeswoman was there for us. The doctor came in and sat down. He told us, "Dave has broken his back at the eighth vertebrae, his spinal cord is severed and two vertebrae are crushed. He will never walk again. His lungs are punctured, we are not certain about brain damage, and possibly there are internal injuries. We will need to stabilize him in order to do surgery to place metal rods in his back. I cannot do the surgery myself, as my wrist is in this cast, but another orthopedic surgeon will do it, most likely on Monday (three days away)." He asked if we had any questions, which he answered and then left. I was in complete shock, numb, but acutely aware of everything around me. My senses were so heightened it was painful. I remember every detail of that waiting time in depth. We made calls to family and to our pastor. Eventually Dave was moved to the ICU (Intensive Care Unit) on the third floor, where we could very briefly see him again. Family, friends, and our pastor began to arrive. The sadness was so intense, and it was commonly felt by all present, but the assurance of love was everywhere, and the agonizing time of waiting was just beginning.

My gratitude journal for that day reads: Thank you God, Dave is alive! Thank you for Kelly, dear Kelly, and Archie, strong Archie. Thank you for helicopters, medical professionals, Reverend Bill. Thank you for Kim's and Robbie's voices on my answering machine, offering their love and concern.

Our pastor, Reverend Bill arrived, as did family members and friends. We all sat frozen in time, filled with fear and apprehension, in the waiting room. A few of the family were able to see Dave briefly. He was in so much pain and under such heavy medication that it was hard to tell if he knew us. It pained us to leave, but we had to return home for the many items we needed. Archie left for home at 10 P.M., and I left with Reverend Bill at 2 A.M.

The next morning I was with Benjamin and Emily, and Kelly's parents were with her. They stayed at a motel next to the hospital. All morning the kids and I talked about their Dad being injured as we played and rode our bikes. At one point in the morning a farm stand customer and his wife came to my front door (Mr. and Mrs. Magoun) with one hundred dollars for Dave. He told me of a World War II experience he had and how people helped him, and so he wanted to help Dave. What a dear and precious thing for them to do. Archie and I returned to U Mass Medical Friday afternoon. Dave was now in a private room on the floor. When he was awake we were to ask him questions and show him pictures to help him mentally. I would say, "Do you know who I am?" and he would answer, "My mother" or "My Mom." After three times of asking him this same question, interspersed with other questions and long spans of time and consciousness, I asked him again, "Who am I?" and he said, "Helen Coll. You're my mother!" Well, I didn't ask that question again! It was funny and reassuring, for I then knew for sure he did not receive brain damage from the hit on the head. I told him about the Magouns and he could not believe they would do that for him. Later he asked me to tell him the story again. He was very touched by their caring and sympathy, and he didn't even know them.

All during this time Dave was in a restrained position, on his back, in a special tilting bed; it turned side to side to relieve pressure on his back and helped his body to drain better. We were supposed to keep him as quiet as possible and not let him move his head or arms. The first 24 hours he was still on the rescue board they carried him out of the woods on, and the pressure of the hard board had caused his skin to breakdown at the base of his spine (the coccyx area). This was not a major concern then, but later became a large obstacle in his recovery process.

Kelly's cousin, Cindy, came each day to the hospital and sat quietly and worked on a needlework project. She was a very comforting and reassuring presence. She was better able to hear than we were at times, and would remember details we had missed. She was an invaluable asset over the two weeks we were at U Mass Medical. Her unassuming presence and strong faith were so consoling.

Dave had a hemo-pneumothroax because his lungs were collapsed and wounded, meaning there was blood present and the lungs were not inflated. And so he had three (chest) tubes to drain the fluid from his injured lungs and lung cavity, and these were each hooked to a pleural evac (water seal) drainage system. This is a closed system so that no air or fluid can go from the container (system) back into the lungs. After days of listening to the water bubbling in the pleural vacs he kept asking, "When is the water man coming?" He also had a tube for oxygen, a stomach tube, and a catheter tube. He was hooked to monitors for heart and breathing rates. The days were long, but the nights were longer. We never left Dave alone; someone of the family was always with him to see to his needs and keep in contact with the nurses and doctors. The nursing staff got to know us and we them. They were very good to Dave and to us.

We were now waiting for Dave's body and lungs to stabilize so surgery could be done. It was scheduled for Monday morning. He had three days to wait with our help. As time passed it was growing harder and harder to keep him calm and quiet. He knew us but when we asked, "Where are you?" or "Do you know what happened to you?" he would answer, "You tell me I'm in the hospital, but I don't remember coming here." He did not and still does not have any memory of the accident or of the days before and a few days after surgery. The more time that went by before the surgery, the more agitated Dave became. He pulled out one of one chest tubes (it had to be put back in), and he also pulled out the blood transfusion lines several times, and this was with his hands tied to the bed sides. He was very strong. During the times I was with him I would quietly talk with him, my head next to his, stroking his hair, and when he was particularly agitated I would sing to him. Most songs made me cry so I would hum them. The song that seemed to comfort him and myself the most was *Kumbaya; O Lord (Come By Here Oh Lord)*. When I stopped singing he would make, "Um, um" sounds, for me to continue. When I did he would be peaceful again. Over and over I prayed The Lord's Prayer, Psalm 23, a special prayer I had written years ago that gives me comfort and blessed assurance, and I had many conversations with God.

Monday morning finally arrived, but only after the longest weekend of our lives. They took Dave down for his surgery and they allowed Kelly and me to accompany him to the holding area before surgery because we were quieting influences for him. We watched as they wheeled him into surgery and then began our vigil along with Dave's sister Peggy, Reverend Bill, family, and friends in the chapel of the hospital and the waiting room. It took many hours but finally his doctor came to waiting room to tell us of the surgery. He had placed two 12 inch titanium metal rods along side Dave's vertebrae to stabilize it and the spinal cord. He told us the spinal cord was not severed (miracle number 3) and that the dura (the covering of the spinal cord) was intact and no spinal fluid had leaked. I wanted to touch him, hug him. I thought he was Godlike at that moment. We were all very happy and felt this was very good news. We cried through our smiles and everyone hugged each other. The extreme tensions of the last four days were beginning to ease. When Dave was moved to the recovery room Kelly and I were allowed to go down and be with him again, to help him remain calm. It also helped us to feel useful and needed and to be close to Dave.

The next few days were a slow process of Dave's post-op recovery, and gradually they were able to remove his chest tubes one at a time, over a few days. The day the last one was to come out, Archie and I were in the room visiting with Dave. The young doctor came in and said, "I'm here to remove your last chest tube." Dave said, "Okay." I looked at Archie in alarm, for I knew what was about to happen. These chest tubes are very large and must be pulled out forcefully. The doctor opened and prepared the removal and dressing kit, and I felt it shouldn't be open to the air for so long because of germs that might be in the air. I whispered to Archie what was about to happen and stood at Dave's bedside praying that the removal site not become infected. The doctor said at the count of three Dave should take a deep breath and hold it while he pulled out the tube. "One, two, three, hold." He pulled it out. Dave yelled, "Ow! Don't do that again!" Fortunately for him he had no recollection (due to pain medication) of the last two times the tubes were pulled out, nor does he remember this one. The next morning I was home eating my breakfast and I felt something on my right side. I went and looked in the mirror and there was a large (size of the head of a tack) sore with a white purulent head on it surrounded by red skin. I could not believe my eyes. I did not have it before and here it was on the same side and same location as the tube that was removed from Dave the day before. I have heard of sympathetic pain but never experienced it. I hesitated telling Archie about the sore, for I felt he might not believe me, but finally I did and I showed it to him while we were driving to Worcester that afternoon to visit Dave. He said, "My ribs on that side have been hurting me today." I said, "That isn't funny." He said, "I'm serious, they really have been hurting." I believed him. Others told me of their experiences with Dave's injury, and that they too experienced pain and soreness. One man felt pain in his back at the location of Dave's surgery and at the same time as his surgery. Another woman had a sore on her back in the same area as Dave and it lasted a long time and left just before Dave's healed. Coincidences? I do not think so. I now believe we can help people by carrying some of their pain and suffering, that we are connected in ways not totally understood by humankind.

After the surgery Dave had to be fitted for a full upper-body brace called a "turtle shell: to support his spine until it healed. It was a molded plastic brace which covered his entire chest and back and was held on by Velcro tapes. He had to wear this brace all summer, through the hot weather. It was very uncomfortable but very necessary. He spent two weeks at U Mass Medical until it was time to move onto a rehabilitation hospital. Kelly, Gus (Kelly's dad), and

Cultivating Life
A Story of Earth and Hearth

I checked out one in Massachusetts and interviewed another, but they were not acceptable for Dave. They did not allow family to play a strong role in the patient's daily therapy or accommodate overnight stays. We had been with Dave everyday and night and wanted to have a major role in his rehabilitation as well. Through friends of Kelly's, Craig Hospital in Denver, Colorado, was located, and it was decided that that was the best place for Dave to go, because they specialize in spinal cord injury. A private jet was hired by Kelly's parents, Linda and Gus, and Archie and I, to fly him there. The morning of his departure arrived, and the children, Kelly's parents and Archie all came to see Dave off with Kelly and I accompanying him, along with a male nurse. What a surprise to read his name on his shirt! (Jesus Baridas) Kelly said, "Do you believe it, Dave? Jesus is flying us to Colorado!" It was a perfect flight (except Kelly and I were not allowed to go to the bathroom for the entire flight!) Guess what we did the moment the Lear jet landed?

Denver is the mile-high city and high altitude presented a problem the first few days. We combated it with large glasses of ice water. It really helps. The ambulance took us all to the hospital. My first impression was: this is not a place for my son, he can't be this injured, but that thought left my mind immediately. They were so positive, compassionate, capable, and accommodating. I knew moments later this was the best place for Dave to recover and learn to live his life to the fullest. Kelly and I were to stay in an apartment provided by the hospital for family of patients. I remember writing to Archie, "There are times I look around and wonder, Where am I? It is hard to believe life has changed so much and we find ourselves now on a different course altogether."

My favorite college professor, George Flavin and his wife Claudia had moved to Denver in November 1998 so I called them up. George came over the next day to take Kelly and me to do some shopping and acquaint us with the area. Isn't it strange that George was there to help me in this my hour of great need (miracle number 4). He and Claudia were so willing and helpful all during our stays. We found ourselves surrounded at the hospital by many other families going through the same thing we were, and Dave saw many people in the same situation as himself but in varying degrees of ability. The staff of nurses, therapists, and doctors were the very best. They welcomed Dave and us into every aspect of his care. Benjamin, Emily, and Gus arrived a few days after we got there and then we all lived in an apartment provided for us. We took part in all of Dave's therapy sessions and classes. He had physical therapy, occupational therapy, recreational therapy, speech therapy, tests for brain damage (Dave strongly disliked these for he was fine in that respect), but they needed to assess any damage he might have incurred. He attend classes from 9 A.M. to 4 P.M. five days a week. I made note in my journal one day, "His eyes seem to tell the story of how he feels more than anything. They change day to day, but his smile remains and his positive attitude as well. He has a long road to go down but no one knows what is at the end of it for him. He is very courageous and strong and compassionate to others."

Two days after the children arrived in Colorado it was Father's Day and we celebrated with a cookout at the Friendship House of the hospital. This is a house complete with kitchen, dining room, living room, bathroom, television, VCR, porch, barbecue—everything to make you feel at home. Of course, all of it is wheelchair accessible. All we had to do was sign up for the time period we wanted to use it. You could sign for 12-3, 3-6, or 6-9. Dave was now sitting up in a wheelchair and was able to support his head. Regaining some normalcy was the order of the afternoon.

Dave has always been a very hard worker, but now he had to work harder than ever before and I am proud to say he was "up for the job" and doing very well. He began by working on skills to increase his upper body strength but was slowed some by his broken right shoulder, leaving only his left arm to lift his body weight until the break healed. His spirit and motivation were inspiring to all around him.

The next weekend Archie arrived. His plane was late and I fell to pieces when I found out his plane was going to be delayed. I could not wait to see him. When he did arrive we literally fell into each others arms and had to hold each other up, which we couldn't really do, so we sat down right there in the waiting area and held on and cried for a long time. It was the most emotional time of our lives, bar none. I was so happy to have him to hold on to and talk with, and yes, laugh as well as cry with. That Sunday afternoon Archie and I had Dave all to ourselves, as Kelly, the children and her parents were gone to a very well deserved time off. We went outside to the beautiful grassed yard where there was a fish pond and benches and various patios. For me the most touching sight happened that day. Dave had to have weight transfers every fifteen minutes to relieve the pressure on his bottom. We had to tip back his wheelchair into our lap and he would then rest his head on our shoulder for five minutes. That afternoon Archie was doing the weight transfers and it was so poignant to see their heads next to each other and them talking quietly together.

By this time I was living in a motel a few miles away, and the children would come to sleep over and swim in the pool and use the hot tub. Archie and the kids were with me that weekend and it was so good to have them there. We again had a cookout at the Friendship house, as we continued to do many weekends. I had been there for two weeks when I left to go home with Archie for the next two weeks. I was very so grateful Gus was there to look after and help everyone.

Back home in Jaffrey everybody was sending their love and prayers to Dave. My niece, Beth, and sisters-in-law, Carmen and Cathie, started and were busy managing the David Coll and Family Fund for those people who wanted to contribute money to help Dave. They put out cans for donations in local stores and businesses, and also people mailed checks to them and to us most everyday. Such an amazing outpouring of love and support. It touched all of us very deeply, but we did not tell Dave about it for a while. He is very proud and would find it difficult to accept financial help. Eventually we told him, and when he adjusted to the idea he too was very humbled and appreciative. Kelly and Dave's home was in need of remodeling to make it accessible for him and his wheelchair. Beth's husband, Norman, and Dave's brother, Mark, spearheaded the construction job and Beth and Carmen organized the packing up and cleaning up. Archie took videos of the progress to bring to Dave on his next trip to Colorado. All summer I would be home two weeks and then return to Colorado for another two weeks. This I did three times that summer. Kelly's Mom, Linda, also came out and returned home three times, for she was performing Kelly's work in her absence. Kelly's brother, Travis, and Dave's cousin, David, drove Gus's van out to Colorado, which helped make many area trips possible and saved money on renting a van. Dave's sister, Suzanne, came out for a visit as did my cousin, Barbara. Friends and family of Kelly and Dave also came out to visit him. We tried to maintain strong connections between home (Jaffrey) and hospital throughout his two-and-a-half month stay. A fund raising dance was held on a very hot Saturday night in August. The American Legion donated their building, the band "Kindred" donated their talents, and many raffle items, door prizes, tickets, and food, were also donated. It was a huge success and we were so deeply grateful for the outpouring of love and care. We were truly blessed and sustained by the generosity of so many people.

Earlier I spoke of the sore on the coccyx area of his spine; well, it continued to grow and become a serious problem in his recovery. It would not heal as it should and required special care. He received special E-Stim therapy (an electric stimulator which increases the blood flow to the sore to promote healing) and the application of a very expensive ointment that finally did the trick of healing the area. We had to be very careful to check his skin every day and make sure his clothing did not have bumps or creases to cause redness and open the sore again. When he came home I cut out the back section of the waistband with the belt loop of his jeans, and replaced it with a smooth, single layer of fabric so as to make them as smooth as possible at the site of his sore. It now has a very fragile new skin covering it, and we did not want it to break down again.

In his hospital room he always had a roommate, but the room was fairly large and we would often eat dinner with Dave, family style. I would cook at the apartment or we would order take-out and bring the food to his room, where we set up a folding table Gus had bought and eat with Dave. Another very poignant time for me was when the children and I went over to say goodnight to Dave one night. Emily had been withholding kissing her Dad. This night I had not seen Dave all day and just had to go over to say goodnight. The children asked to come with me. We talked briefly then we all held hands and said our bedtime prayers together. Ben kissed his Dad goodnight and I kissed him and Emily said she too wanted to give him a kiss. It was a very tender and special moment and my eyes and heart were filled with tears of joy. Benjamin was eight and never hesitated a moment with his Dad's injury; he was his biggest supporter and fast becoming a wheelchair expert. He is always very concerned and helpful in every way. He is so emotionally connected to Dave and his feelings that he was able to express them in words and actions. It was more difficult for Emily because she was only six, and this experience was so foreign for her. But as time went on she knew Dave was still her dad and always would be. Both children had times of deep sadness but with their parents' help they have become very compassionate individuals. Dave is the same person now he always has been, and anyone who knows him can see that very plainly. I tell him, he will not be viewed as handicapped but as handicapable, and truly he is. Again from a letter to Archie, "Dave and I had a beautiful time talking this afternoon while the others were gone for a trip. He is very special and loving and will 'fight the good fight.' We are fortunate to have him as our son and I am very grateful for his life. All of us have a lot of faith in God and it is keeping us strong for each other and all that life holds, day by day."

Kelly astonished us with her strength, faith, courage, and unbounding love. She has been there for Dave every step of the way and continues to be there for him and the children, as well as working full time in the family business. Dave has a very positive attitude, beautiful smile, outgoing personality, and enjoys life every day, despite the fact he has pain to contend with every day. They remain a strong and loving family in all areas of their lives. We praise God for all He has blessed us with, and continues to shower upon us. We are eternally grateful for all our friends' and relatives' love, concern, prayers, and undying help. May each of them be blessed in their lives. We will always be there for them as they have been for us. The David Coll and Family Fund raised and astounding $30,000.00! Archie and I personally received over one hundred letters and cards, many with donations in them. One Jaffrey man, Dick, wrote letters and sent postcards to Dave all summer long from England where he was vacationing. It was like we were experiencing, right along with Dick, the adventure he was on. Dave's room was full of cards and posters. One large card Bill had everyone sign at Mrs. Murphy's Donut Shop. Dave loves their coffee and in fact they sent him some while he was in Colorado. So many people remembered him with cards and gifts, some of whom he did not even know.

I remember one weekend when Beth and Norman and Barbara were visiting, I cooked a roast turkey dinner and loaded it into a shopping cart Gus had found.

Cultivating Life
A Story of Earth and Hearth

We wheeled it from the apartment to the outdoor garden area and ate dinner outdoors. It was a wonderful day. We repeated it (different menu) the following weekend when Archie and Linda were out for a visit once again. Beth and Norman were there to talk about the house remodeling plans. The Friendship House served as a fine example of what could be accomplished as well as the complete wheelchair-friendly kitchen that was in the hospital's occupational therapy room. Patients would work in the kitchen preparing meals and get a feel for accessibility. One assignment for Dave was to plan a meal, shop for it, and then prepare it! The therapy departments thought of every aspect of living and gave patients the experiences to cope. One day they went to a mall and Dave proceeded to ride the escalators, to the amazement of some people and the surprise of others. Another day they were out on the city sidewalks to learn to go up and down curbs and steps! It is marvelous what people can accomplish while in a wheelchair with some training and a lot of effort. That is where patience and perseverance come to play, and Dave has both.

From time to time we all needed breaks from the hospital routine and we would go out for dinner or bike riding or white-water rafting. Gus had a relative, John, who took rafts down the Arkansas River, and the children went three times during the summer. They loved it! I had the pleasure of joining them once and it was thrilling. I would go again anytime. The children and Kelly also did some horseback riding. George and Claudia took me for drives up into the Rocky Mountains, to Red Rocks Amphitheater, and to see the Denver sights. Such gorgeous scenery in Colorado. The children, Gus, Suzanne, and I went to Colorado Springs to visit the Garden of the Gods and to see the Indian Cliff Dwellings. Gus was wonderful with the children. He kept them busy and entertained as well as doing laundry, shopping and housework. They did many interesting things together. I wanted to stay close by Dave and Kelly and so I enjoyed going to playgrounds and riding bikes with them.

After a while Dave was also going out on trips. The recreational therapy department had many trips for patients and families to enjoy. I was very apprehensive when they talked about going white-water rafting or boating or hot-air ballooning, etc. but I understood they were trying to have patients think about what they like to do and let them know they can achieve these goals once again, possibly with special equipment, but that they can do whatever they set their minds to do. At the hospital there is a five story parking garage where Dave would push his wheelchair to the top floor and then "fly" down! How he could do it, I don't know. I could hardly walk up it. He had to learn to drive with hand controls and I had the pleasure of going with him that first time out in a car. I was very relaxed and he was in complete control. It was wonderful to see him driving once again. One night we went out to play miniature golf and Dave won, fair and square against all of us.

Each of these achievements made me regard ability and disability from different perspectives than I ever before. To this day Archie and I are both very changed persons, and for the better. We now see life through different eyes. We are acutely aware of the lack of accessibility for those individuals having to live their life in wheelchairs. The Americans with Disabilities Act has now been in force since July 1990. It states America's commitment to full and equal opportunity for all citizens, including the 53 million Americans with disabilities. The act reflects the American ideals which value the many contributions individuals can make and helps them to realize their full potential. But the reality is; the vast majority of businesses, parking lots, sidewalks, doorways, etc., are not accessible for wheelchairs. Dave is constantly coming across places he cannot get to or enter—from friends' homes to restaurants and stores. It is very frustrating and businesses and people should be made to comply with the law. Suzanne heard a program on TV advocating that all new home construction should be done with accessibility in mind. I agree one hundred per cent. During construction it is just as easy to make a doorway 32 inches, create bathrooms and kitchens with open area under the sinks, and construct ramps to enter houses instead of steps. Too many people are being cut off and held back from living fully attainable lives, and this needs to be changed now. Insurance companies have a long way to go in helping disabled persons. They put obstacle after obstacle in the way, hoping people will give up and not pursue the medicine, equipment, and everyday needs they should and in many cases must have. One day shortly after Dave came home, I was returning equipment to a medical supply place. They had sent the wrong shower seat, toilet seat, and wheelchair. They were for an elderly person not a wheelchair-bound person. As I unloaded the equipment from my car a woman came out and said, "You are not just going to leave this here, are you?" I said, "No. I am just unloading my car and then I will bring everything into your store." She went back in and waited for me to come in, never offering any help. I was very pleasant in telling her about what I was returning and why, and then asked her, "When will your business get it right? Dave is not elderly, he is disabled. He cannot use just any shower bench or toilet seat or wheelchair or cushion. He must have ones specifically ordered by his doctor and designed for his needs." She apologized and said she would order the proper equipment. She did call back the next day and say they would be getting the correct equipment in soon. Of course Dave needed it immediately, and we had doctor's orders for them earlier so that they would be here and ready when he arrived home. They (Kelly and Dave) have since changed their medical supply company. This is just a small example of the battles that have to take place in order for patients to obtain their necessary health care needs. Patients are not always in the position to do this haggling; they need advocates to help them, but many do not have anyone. I feel every patient should be entitled to their own personal advocate, if they do not have family or friends that serve in this capacity for them. I cannot imagine someone not having family to help them if they find themselves in a similar situation to Dave's. Life would be just too difficult and challenging without someone to help them. I know social services try to do all they can, but they to are too busy to give the necessary time and attention each individual's needs.

New Hampshire Vocational Rehabilitation has been very helpful in supplying Dave with equipment to aid him in his vocation. They helped provide an Easy Riser seat for his truck; this seat he slides onto from his wheelchair and then it hydraulically rises to the level of his truck seat, so he can then transfer to it with use of a slide board. They also helped provide him obtain a Freedom Lift for his truck. This is a lift that is mounted in the back body of his truck, which Dave can operate from hand controls. It has a long arm that swings out and around to allow Dave and his wheelchair get onto a platform, so he can then have access to do jobs at heights he would not be able to otherwise reach. Each state has laws that obligate them to provide handicapped persons the access needed to return then to their jobs(vocation). If your state refuses to provide a disabled person with the needed equipment for them to return to their vocation, get the agency to put it in writing that they refuse your request. Most likely they will come through and provide what it is you need; if they do not, you have an appeals process you can go through to get them to comply.

Throughout our time in Colorado we had the pleasure of witnessing magnificent sunrises and glorious sunsets; viewing purple mountains majesties with snow-capped peaks in July; and the vast expanse of the prairie and plains; wondering at lightning as bright as florescent bulbs ready to break; hearing new birds singing their lovely songs; watching with renewed interest the squirrels feeding and playing; and observing the smiles and tears of friends and strangers alike. We made many new friends from faraway places, struggling with their own crisis but willing to share in ours. The doctors, nurses, therapists and staff always gave their professional best as well as their personal love, tears, and smiles. We were on and still continue this marvelous journey called life with newfound appreciation of its fragility and the courage required to live fully. None of us will ever be the same—we are now different, changed, but humbled by the presence of loving and caring professionals; prayerful and vigilant communities; and steadfast family and friends, who literally carried us by their prayers, each day of our journey.

As time approached for Dave to come home, he expressed concern, doubts and fears about how it would be to be back home. That was very normal and I would reassure him that all he can do is take life one day at a time. Imagine, he had come a long way; originally we could only think of one hour at a time and now we were talking one day at a time. I (and everyone) would tell him, "You came this far, this well and this soon, so anything is possible. You have what it takes to do whatever you want and need to do."

The remodeling of Dave's house was now in full swing. Volunteers showed up, local businesses made donations of materials and contractors of their labor. Plumbing, electrical, driveway and sidewalk paving, bulldozing and backhoe work, fill, grass and plants, new cabinets and bathroom fixtures, painting, moving, cleaning, everything that needed to be done to make the home wheelchair-friendly was completed, just in the knick of time for Dave, Kelly, Benjamin, and Emily to arrive from the airport on August 27, 1999. Many family members went to Logan Airport in Boston to meet them and escort them to Jaffrey. All the way up the hill to their home were large yellow ribbons tied around many trees and a huge sign was hung from the barn welcoming them back. It was a great night!

Later in September Kelly and Dave gave a thank you barbecue for the many volunteers who helped with the remodeling project. There was a pig roast done by Jeff and chicken barbecue done by Archie. Kelly and Dave gave golden hammers to Norman and Mark. It was a wonderful celebration, but the best part was that Dave and family were home at last in small-town Jaffrey, where people rally around and help their neighbors when they are in need. As Kelly said, "We are so blessed. David's been here all of his life, and when something happens, people pull together. They work together, from people at the church sending cards (like faithful Mildred) and prayers, to people working on the house, to people dropping off food. Just unbelievable! It made it so nice to come home to!"

Dave is still in a wheelchair and we are still praying for THE miracle, but we have great hopes for his future. Dave has traveled a long road, not only in miles but spiritually as well. He is my inspiration and my hero. He possess great courage and a positive attitude. Whenever I am down or faced with a difficulty or pain, I immediately think of Dave and tell myself, "If he can do it(endure), I can too." There is a saying I heard one time, "Pain is inevitable, but suffering is optional." Christopher Reeve wrote in an article I read, "If someone were to ask me what is the most difficult lesson I've learned from (being paralyzed), I'm very clear about it: I know I have to give when sometimes I really want to take."

Kelly has given and continues to give so much to Dave, Ben, and Emily and thus to all of our family. She is the "unsung hero" of Dave's accident and we desire recognition for her as well as Dave. She is also courageous, brave, forbearing, and loving; and we know great things will come to her through this life-changing and enlightening experience. Proverbs 31:10 & 11 says: "A good wife who can find? She is far more precious than jewels. The heart of her husband trusts in her, and he will have no lack of gain." 28 & 29: "Her children rise up and call her blessed; her husband also, and he praises her: 'Many women have done excellently, but you surpass them all.'" We sincerely thank you and give you our heartfelt appreciation and recognition of all you are. Kelly you are an "Earth Angel", and you are loved!

It is now exactly two years from Dave's injury. He returned to Craig Hospital last summer and is scheduled to go again this summer for reevaluation and updates in care. In December 2000 he had surgery to remove the two titanium rods from his back. The surgery went fine and he was home in two days. The doctor was now able to obtain a clear MRI (Magnetic Resonance Image, a type of x-ray) of his spine. He found the spinal cord is still compressed at the sight of his injury, but the healing process looked good. He has not gained any movement but we remain hopeful. Recently Dave and Kelly purchased a large lot of land and are planning to build a new home on it. Where they presently live, the yard is not accessible for him. It is all uphill and downhill and rough terrain. At the new home he will be able to mow his own lawn and be able to go out-of-doors easier, something he truly loves to do. He will not have to worry about rolling downhill on the ice in winter. It will be closer to his work and the children's school, and I think he will take great pride in completing this huge project independently. He has already done much of the excavating work using an ax handle to work the foot pedals of the excavator. It is hard to keep a good man down, and who would ever want to? Go for it, Dave! Do and be all you can be!

Life can change in an instant, material things no longer matter, the only important thing is today; not yesterday, not tomorrow, but today—the here and now. If your life changes drastically, in an instant—pray you have the inner strength and spirit to live—in the here and now moments of your life. We all continue to be blessed everyday we live, with friends who care and show their concern by words and actions. May we be able to live our lives as a tribute to everyone who helped us and believed in us. We are eternally grateful for our families and friends love, care, prayers, and undying help. May each of them be blessed in their lives and may we will always be there for them. We now are looking forward with tremendous joy, strong faith, abiding hope, enduring love, filled hearts and humble gratitude to many bright and happy tomorrows.

After a tragedy has occurred, the first stage you encounter is shock, disbelief. You are in crisis and everything has changed, including the roles you play. Next comes the adjustment time. You feel out of control, powerless, full of anger. You then need to gain information so as to be in command and be able to manage once again. Then you need to be accepting and to reach out to others, ask for help, keep in touch. All these I read in a book about tragedy. I know we moved through all the various stages very quickly after Dave's tragic accident, and I will tell you why we progressed so rapidly and did not stay in any stage for very long.

Helen Coll

Our love of God and faith in Him and hope for tomorrow completely sustained us and comforted us and brought us through to the light! Praise be the Lord!

Cultivating Life
A Story of Earth and Hearth

Ray, Suzanne, Reuben, Ryan—2001

Mark, Lori, Joshua—2001

Above: Whitney, Lyndsey, Peggy, Paul, Isaac & Abbie—2001

Left: Ben, Dave, Kelly, & Emily—2001.

Cultivating Life
A Story of Earth and Hearth

**Left: Helen and Archie Coll
2001**

**Below: Archie Coll Family
2001**

CHAPTER FIFTEEN

THE FUTURE

"Two roads diverged in the wood, and I—I took the one less traveled by,
And that has made all the difference."

Robert Frost

As with Frost, the road I took was not only the "the one less traveled by," it also "made all the difference" and was the right road for me, and probably the only road I could have taken and been so fulfilled and known such happiness.

Archie and I are now in a position to take some "time off." We both enjoy traveling and look forward to seeing many new places and things from a different light and in a fresh perspective. We anticipate seeing more of this wonderful country of ours (The United States of America) as well as other countries. We have journeyed to The Netherlands to see where my paternal Dutch ancestors (the Van Blarcoms) lived and to Ste. Anne de Madawaska, New Brunswick, Canada, to visit the Sirois family (Archie's maternal) homeland. We intend on traveling go to Germany, where Archie's paternal family (Koull) originated nine generations ago, and venture to England, the birthplace of my grandfather Woodbury (maternal side of family). I have been transacting genealogical studies for many years and find it exciting to trace both of our families. I have found many interesting and some profound commonalties. We prefer each other's company and take pleasure in auto driving holidays and what they reveal to us in patterns and possibilities not apparent in our day-to-day lives, which are full of concerns. Now we hope we may be fortunate to live long enough to achieve some of our dreams and goals for travel and our retirement years.

What is the future of this farm and of agriculture? No one really knows. But as to our farm, we have taken steps to pass on this operation to our son Mark who has a son, Joshua, who at the age of eleven is interested in farming. As I said before, it will be the first time it has passed from one generation to another. That in itself will be a big accomplishment in this day and age, especially here in New England. Archie once said, "We will always have agriculture, for it is necessary for life," but where will agricultural lands and operations remain vital?

Turning over a business one has built and carefully nurtured for 40+ years is not a simple or easy thing to execute; quite the contrary, it is a very complex endeavor. More families fail in their attempts than succeed. And there are many ways of completing a transition, but this is how we are achieving it.

Cultivating Life
A Story of Earth and Hearth

First and foremost, a son or daughter must be interested in assuming an operation, and our son Mark is ready and willing. Secondly, the parents have to be agreeable to relinquishing the business, and that is what we are in process of attaining now. Our son has worked on the farm for years and this needs to be considered in the total picture of the "takeover." We, the parents, have put in many years of hard work, sometimes doing without financial benefit, especially in the early years. We worked long hours that certainly we have not received monetary payment for ("sweat equity"), but which we have gained personal satisfaction from. We have done without days off and vacations and have had debt load from time to time in order to expand the business, build buildings, buy equipment and animals and feed. A great deal of our "pay" over the years has been in living the lifestyle we chose for the sake of raising our family. Living on a farm has enabled us to be self-employed and to pursue our own aspirations, goals, and dreams. We are now in the first year of a five-year transition time. It is difficult, to say the least, to let go of a business we have created, but on the other hand, we are fortunate to have Mark ready and very capable of accomplishing this. We cannot keep it forever. We have raised each of our children to be independent, business minded individuals, achievers in whatever it is they chose to attain. Now Archie and I must lead from hearts and not control from our heads. We have every confidence in Mark and Lori and faith in our past guidance and leadership.

Over the years we have had to continually educate ourselves and keep abreast of the latest agricultural trends as to new innovations and marketing opportunities. We have had to hone management skills, to say nothing of keeping up-to-date on government laws, programs, requirements, and regulations. We are always reading and taking courses to be aware of the latest farm practices.

Archie and I have been and continue to be members of many organizations. Among them are: American Farm Bureau Federation as well as our state and county Farm Bureau, New Hampshire Poultry Growers Association (past president), New Hampshire Vegetable Growers Association (past president), and United Cooperative Farmers, Inc.(past president). Archie was on the national Farm Bureau Young Farmers board for two years and traveled to several states to attend conventions or conferences. It was a special learning experience early in our farm careers. For seven years he was on the Jaffrey Planning Board. It takes a lot of dedication to be active in associations while working long hours seven days a week, but the benefits have been many. You get to meet people with like interests and experiences, see other parts of the state and country, find out the latest practices, products, seeds, and equipment that are available, and speak with experts in these various field enterprises. The Cooperative Extension has always been there with invaluable assistance. If we have any problem or question, they will find out the answer. Over the years their expertise has been priceless. Reading agricultural periodicals is another source of continuing education on the very latest technology available to us.

On May 11, 1999, we were recognized by the Jaffrey Grange No. 135 as Community Citizens of the Year in recognition of "outstanding service to our community and mankind, and for dedication and personal involvement which are gratefully and sincerely acknowledged." A tribute we were humbled by. It was a very enjoyable as well as a surprise evening for us that was attended by our family and friends.

We always need to be aware of new innovations and seek marketing opportunities to help ensure continuing success. I attended computer classes and business management courses, learned bookkeeping skills as well as software programs to do the necessary bookwork. We incorporated our business for reasons of transferring ownership successfully, continually take classes given through the Cooperative Extension Service for farmers in fields related to our operation—growing and culture of sweet corn, strawberries, small vegetable crops, flowers, greenhouse operation, estate planning, and all aspects of agribusiness. We also attend seminars and conference meetings of Farm Bureau Federation—county, state, and national levels—to keep abreast of legislative issues and testifying when necessary. Being ever-vigilant as to changes which might or could affect us in our business life is imperative.

In all of our years of farming we have never had any farm subsidies paid to us and we have always operated without any price supports or financial aid from anyone.

Now it is Mark and Lori's turn to manage this farm. They will do things their way—not ours. They are now faced with many of the same issues and circumstances we were faced with, but much of the groundwork is completed. Success had been ours over the years and hopefully they will experience success as well. Everyone sees life through different eyes and makes decisions as to what and how they see. One is not right or wrong, better or worse; they are just different. We believe in Mark and Lori and know they will succeed in all they do!

We have always felt that we are plowing the fields of our farm not only to provide food for people today, but also for all those who come after us. We hope to keep good, fresh, healthful food coming to local people and to keep our fields open and fertile, so as to provide a living for our family and maintain a pastoral view for all who pass by to enjoy. As John Muir said, "Everyone needs beauty, as well as bread...," Farms provide everyone with green, growing, changing scenery and restful vistas.

Many people have a "romantic" impression of farm life. To a very minor extent this may be true, but the realistic view is that of dedication to something

Cultivating Life
A Story of Earth and Hearth

requiring attention 24 hours a day, 365 days a year. It can create worry today as well as provide hope for tomorrow. When I married my farmer, I was still "wet behind the ears" about what I was in for. It is a "package deal"—the farmer and the farm—and it is at times a love/hate package for me. I love the idea of living on a farm and raising our children here and having the sun shining and the corn growing and the hens laying, but I hate it when there hasn't been rain for a weeks and storms come and wreck what we have growing and the temperature is 90° in the shade and everything becomes all-consuming. I lived 13 years in rural a community in New Jersey, where we had our days off and vacations. But when I moved to New Hampshire and married a farmer we no longer had the luxury of days off and vacations waited for many years. I often had to make trade-offs in my mind to keep on farming. Being a farm wife is all about caring, supporting, listening, and always being there, especially when the times are tough.

Why should we (the collective population) be concerned about saving farmland? Archie says, "We should preserve farmland for the future of agriculture and for us to continue to be a food-producing country." It is a link between all of us and the past, and we need to save those memories and stories. The stories are of farmers, their wives, and their families diligently working the land, day in and day out, with their own hands, minds, and hearts. With the stories about growing crops, how it is done, by whom, and where, helps bring to form a relationship with the foods we eat. From this knowledge we are able to feed not only our bodies but our hearts and minds. When you save farmland you are saving scenic views, vistas, open greenspace for all to enjoy. It is for the esthetics—the colors of every season of the year. Some call it saving art. Certainly artists enjoy painting pastoral scenes; many do just that from our hillside all seasons of the year. Saving farmland is all about doing something right! This bring to mind the following:

Haiku
Twenty-one houses
Planted on many acres
Cannot be eaten.

Lynn Eschbach, Greenwood Village, CO

Oh, how true! Think of the farmland that has been taken and planted with houses! Here in New England, and in the Midwest, "the breadbasket of the world," and in Florida and California, the states that feed us all, especially in the winter months. Many farm acres now have houses, malls, schools, factories, and more growing on them. Each year, almost two million acres of cropland, pasture, and rangeland are being lost. Once this precious farmland is taken it cannot be returned to productivity. The message is clear: we must do much more to conserve our very vital agricultural land. THINK before voting to take precious, fertile, agricultural land just because it is open and flat. Development should be on land not suitable for farming—for you cannot eat houses and everyone eats at least three times a day, we hope. According to George Lardner reporting in the Washington Post, January 2000; "A HUD report says, "land is being consumed at twice the rate of population growth. From 1994 to 1997, U. S. land consumption increased by 2 percent, but population grew by just 1 percent annually." When farmland is covered with asphalt or built on, its scenic qualities are gone as well as its natural habitat and they are replaced by higher taxes as local governments strive to provide the services needed to these areas, often outside of the central communities, where it is more costly to provide for them. How do we preserve it? In some states the development rights are purchased so as to keep land open and producing. Ronald Jager and Grace Jager write in their book, *The Granite State, New Hampshire*, "In New Hampshire in 1950 there were 13,391 farms and in 2000 there were approximate 3,000."

When development comes to a rural area, farmers have to compete with many more pressures. New neighbors may not like the odors, the noise, and the dust that come from even the best-managed farm.

I know this is a complex issue, more than I can study in depth within this memoir, but still I implore people to STOP and THINK about the food they eat. It doesn't get to the supermarkets if farmers are out of production! Everyone's quality of life suffers, but it is not inevitable. We, collectively must have a different vision of the future, a future with balance, keeping places to grow food and wonderful open spaces for future generations to enjoy by locating developments in areas not already open and close to services they need. Farmers cannot achieve the vision alone. We need conservation organizations and bureaucrats (town, state, national), all supporting protection through commitment and action.

An article I once read authored by Victor Hansen stated; "Family farms are vanishing. The Jeffersonian idea that a man and his family might live on their inherited ground, stay rooted as citizens of their local community, and pass on their land to the next generation may likely disappear in this country...Today less than one percent of the American population earns a living by producing food. Even fewer of these men and women operate family farms." This is true but how could this happen? Food production is now a worldwide proposition. Yields per acre continually increase. The chemical companies are working hard to manufacture more and better herbicides and pesticides. Genetic researchers constantly make possible more productive species. Our dinner tables can have food from all over the globe on them daily. American farmers are now competing with growers in South America, Africa, Australia, and many other countries. The southern hemisphere enjoys summer when we are experiencing winter and thus we can have fresh strawberries as well as other fruits and vegetables all year round.

Time is moving on, but it is my sincere hope that it is not too late to save the remaining family farms for all to benefit from.

In the fall of 1998 I participated in an academic study: The Traditions and Cultures Institute on Martha's Vineyard. I had the opportunity of exploring the rich heritage of an island culture and I completed my learning experience with a personal study entitled: Why And How Has Displacement And Dispossession Occurred For The Wampanoag Indians And For The Agricultural Community On Martha's Vineyard. I found many correlations between the Wampanoags and the farmers, and definitely displacement and/or dispossession occurred for both communities, but here I will speak about the agricultural community. Life on Martha's Vineyard is a microcosm of life in New England. As goes Martha's Vineyard so goes New England? Only time will answer that question. The number of farms on the Vineyard decreased greatly, from twenty dairy farms in 1946 to only one, large commercial farm and a few smaller operations gaining income from farming. Farms have sold due to rising property values. The island has become more tourist oriented, which drives up the land values, especially on an island where land is limited.

Farmland has been displaced by golf courses, resorts, residential and urban development. Farmers have been deprived of their means of earning a living through the increased taxes and temptations of profiting from the sale of their land. Without land you cannot farm. Saving the farmland: feeds people, protects the environment and natural resources and lends beautiful, open views for everyone to enjoy.

There are more similarities than differences between the Vineyard and farming in New Hampshire. One difference is the value of land increased higher on the Vineyard, and that I attribute to the celebrities that have bought land and homes there, plus the fact there is only so much land on an island. The pressures have been greater than we have experienced, but nonetheless the pressures are everywhere, and in order to keep farming sacrifices must be made. These sacrifices are monetary, as well as physical labor.

I had the pleasure of interviewing a farmer, Elisha Smith, born in Oak Bluffs on January 30, 1923, the seventh generation to bear the name Elisha, and his son the eighth. His family has lived on Martha's Vineyard since the 1620s. He was a most interesting man and had many stories to relate of farming and living on the island. Elisha's children, now grow, are not interested in farming. He has one grandson who may want to farm but that remains to be seen. The future for Elisha's farm does not look good. At present he is doing custom farm work such as: plowing and haying for others, as well as caring for his own farm and animals. He no longer does milking. When I asked him about the future of farming on Martha's Vineyard, he told me some of what I already knew from my own experience; the young people today do not want to work the hours and weekends. Over the years the farmers have lost land due to rising property values and taxes, from the influx of residents and tourism. It is sometimes difficult to justify farming when the land may be sold for unbelievable amounts.

I found the changes more dramatic on the Vineyard than on the mainland. The temptations to sell are greater and the prices for land are higher. It is very difficult for agriculture to compete with million dollar homes, golf courses, hotels, etc. This is a free country and we all have choices. Many farmers have yielded to the temptations to sell and I cannot blame them. But for me the rewards of hard work, good living on and from the soil you own, raising a family with animals, and a business to operate, have all been worth everything we have had to do to accomplish a successful family farm. It is very difficult to stop change, be it on an island or the mainland. We do have zoning laws but somehow people can find ways around them. I found it so interesting that many people interviewed for the book *Vineyard Voices* by Linsey Lee enjoyed their earlier lives and still find pleasure living the same way to some extent.

My hopes and dreams for the future of agriculture in New England are to preserve what is left, before it is completely gone from the scene. More than ninety percent of the food we eat in New England is shipped in to us; the only food we produce enough to feed ourselves is milk and apples! Do we want to live on these alone? I think not. The future? If people really value the farms, then they will always be here and I am sure there will be people willing to work them.

I personally do not know a farmer, and I have met many throughout the United States, who intentionally hurts the environment, pollutes the air or water, uses too much fertilizer, pesticides, herbicides (they are too expensive) or does any harm that might endanger himself, his family, or the people he feeds and clothes. Quite the contrary, I find farmers very conscientious, nature-loving, caring, giving people who choose to do without many things in order to live the life they chose and support their families the best they can. I must say here that I personally do not know any mega-agribusiness people and cannot speak to how and what they think and feel, but I can guess the profit line is what matters most to them.

For many children the first animals they learn about are farm animals—the milk-producing Bessie the cow, the egg-laying Henny the Penny, the adorable, pink, Babe the pig, the wise and wonderful Mister Ed the horse. It is a pattern laid down in early childhood—their imagination of animal life. We in this great country of ours need to take a long, hard look at our commitment to preserving our rural life and family farms for the future generations. If we don't, that pattern could become just a figment of our imaginations.

Cultivating Life
A Story of Earth and Hearth

Larry Thompson is quoted saying, "It's not me against them. It's not a line between farmland and cities. It's all of us together, protecting farmland from development by creating higher farm profits within communities thus providing sustained farmland protection." I agree with Thompson and there is more:

It's about good, wholesome, fresh food—for optimal health and well being.
It's about buying locally.
It's about diversification.
It's about good zoning laws.
It's about valuing a lifestyle and preserving it for future generations.
It's about beauty, scenic views to feed the soul.
It's about stewarding the land.
It's about <u>Life</u>!

"Although I die, I shall continue to live in everything that is.
The buffalo eats the grass, and I eat the buffalo;
and when I die, the earth eats me and sprouts more grass.
Therefore, nothing is ever lost, and each thing is in everything, forever."
Chief Luther Standing Bear

APPENDIX

Cultivating Life
A Story of Earth and Hearth

Helen Coll

DEEDS TRACED FOR THIS FARM THROUGH THE REGISTRY

Capt. Peter Powers	1750 (drew the lot)		land	
John Swan	1768 (first settler)		"	
Jacob French	1775		"	
Joseph Danforth	1777		"	
Oliver Carter	1783		"	
Aaron Colman (Eleanor)	1784-93	9 years	"	
Enoch Wellington (Sarah)	1793-99	6 "	"	
John Wood (Sarah) and heirs	1799-1812	13 "	"	&buildings
Laban Ripley (Nancy) and heirs	1812-26	14 "	"	"
David Chamberlain (Abigail)	1826-44	18 "	"	"
James Roberts	1844-45	1 "	"	"
Joseph Turner	1845-46	1 "	"	"
Daniel French (Marietta)	1846-55	9 "	"	"
John Cummings (Mary)	1855-61	6 "	"	"
Samuel W. and Catharine Taggart	1861-64	3 "	"	"
David Malony (Catharine)	1864-70	6 "	"	"
Dexter Pierce (Mary) and heirs	1870-79	9 "	"	"
Orienna and George M. Clark	1879-84	5 "	"	"
Jennie and Edward H. Dillon	1884-99	15 "	"	"
Jules Duval (Roseanna)	1899-1920	21 "	"	"
Frank Hyrk (Hilda)	1920-21	1 "	"	"
Charles and Fannie M. Jurva	1921-54	33 "	"	"
Sydney Woodbury (my grandfather)	1954-57	3 "	"	"
Ruth Van Blarcom (my mother)	1957-61	4 "	"	"
Archie and Helen Coll	1961-present	40+ "	"	"

FROM THE TOWN OF JAFFREY TAX RECORDS

NAME	YEARS	REAL ESTATE improved/unimproved average	ACRES	TOTAL VALUE land & animals	TAX
Cummings	1850	$1080.00		$1275.00	
Taggart	1861-4	1100.00		1444.00	
Malony	1865-7	1000.00		1350.00	
Pierce	1869-79	1070.00		1400.00	$2.96
Clark	1882-4	952.00	(non-resident)		
Dillon	1887-1900	1043.00	125	1579.00	
Duval	1901-19	1175.00	130	1415.00	43.75
Hyrk	1921	1500.00	135	1805.00	64.57
Jurva	1922-56	2000.00	135	3058.00	84.02
Coll	1961-present		49		
Coll	1997		47	205,618.00	7151.39

COMPARISON OF VALUES
(of certain items from inventories and auction)

1818 (auction) Wellington	1858 (inventory) French	1875 (inventory) Pierce
1 cow 23.00	1 cow 35.00	3 cows 75.00
1 colt 60.00	1 colt 75.00	
	1 sleigh 8.00	1 sleigh 2.00
	1 wheelbarrow 1.00	1 wheelbarrow 2.00
1 grindstone 1.80		1 grind stone 2.00
	5 hay forks .75	3 hay forks 1.00
1 feather bed No 1 13.12	4 beds, bedding &	4 beds & bedding 16.00
1 feather bed No 2 10.12	bedstead 39.00	
1 chest 1.75	1 bureau 5.00	1 bureau 1.00
	1 lounge 2.00	1 lounge 2.00
	1 carpet 5.00	1 carpet 2.00
4 tablecloths 3.38	5 tablecloths 2.50	4 tablecloths 1.00
	3 Buffalo robes 8.00	1 Buffalo blanket 2.00
1 looking glass 1.06	4 looking glasses 4.75	
TOTAL ESTATE $2333.00	$3020.00	$1853.00

Helen Coll

LIVESTOCK ON THE FARM
(from tax town tax records)

NAME	YEARS	COWS avg.	HORSES avg.	SHEEP avg.	HOGS avg.
Cummings	1850	9	1		
Taggart	1864	8	1	1	
Malony	1865-67	9	1	4	
Pierce	1869-79	5-8	1	2	10-36
Dillon	1887-1900	1-9	1-3	1-3	2 (2carriages)
Duval	1901-19	1-9	1-2		1-2
Hyrk	1921	2	2		
Jurva	1922-56	5-28	1	1-7	(1944 1 vehicle)
Coll	1961-present	1-2	1	1	(chickens 30,000)

PERSONS IN FARM OPERATIONS IN NEW HAMPSHIRE 1850-1990

YEAR	TOTAL WORKERS	FARM OPERATIONS NUMBER	% OF TOTAL
1850	7,697	4,902	63.7
1870	12,925	6,850	53.0
1900	29,030	10,888	37.5
1920	42,206	11,390	27.0
1930	48,686	10,321	21.2
1940	51,742	8,995	17.4
1950	59,230	6,858	11.6
1960	67,990	4,132	6.1
1970	79,802	2,881	3.6
1980	104,058	2,818	2.7
1990	117,491	2,864	2.4

Cultivating Life
A Story of Earth and Hearth

LAST WILL AND TESTAMENT OF JOHN WOOD
This is the Last Will and Testament of John Wood, July 4, 1799

In the name of God AMEN, the fourth of July in the year of our lord one thousand seven hundred and ninety nine, I John Wood of Jaffrey in the County of Cheshire and the state of New Hampshire, husbandman, being of perfect mind and memory, thanks be to God I here call unto mind the mortality of my body, and knowing that it is appointed for all men to die, Do make and ordain this my last will and testament, That is today principally and first of all, I give and recommend my soul unto the hands of God that gave it, and for my body I recommend it to the earth, to be buried in a Christian like and decent manner at the discretion of my Executor hereafter named. Nothing doubting but at the general resurrection, I shall receive the same again, by the Mighty Power of God. And touching such worldly state wherewith it both pleased God to bless me with this life. I give and bequeath and dispose of the same in the following manner and form.

Impervious, I give and bequeath to John Wood and Eben Wood, my well beloved sons, all my estate both real and personal to be divided between them equally both as to quantity and quality after my just debts and funeral charges are paid out of the estate and I order my two sons John and Eben to pay to Sara Wood my wife and the rest of my heirs the following bequests and legacy.

Item, I order my well beloved wife Sara Wood as long as She remains my widow the east for room and chamber over it as much of the back room and cellar as is necessary for her and that my two sons John and Eben deliver to her yearly for her support, five bushels of Indian corn and five bushels of rye and three bushels of wheat, four weight of beef and one hundred weight of pork and sufficiency of all kinds of sauce and sufficiency of fire wood cut and at the door and the use of one good cow, and two sheep, two barrels of cider, twenty weight of good flax, one pair of good shoes, and to provide for her Necessary Doctoring and Nursing and the use of a good horse and taking to ride at her pleasure. And in case is the in time shall see fit to marry again it shall be considered as a relinquishment of her right to all the above intentioned articles and to her right of dower in my estate, and shall be entitled to five dollars yearly after that out of my estate.

Item, I order my two sons John and Eben to pay to Sally Wood my eldest daughter eighty dollars in money and one two year old heifer in one year after my decease.

Item, I order my said sons to pay unto Hepsibath Wood my second daughter, one hundred dollars in two years after my decease.

Item, I order my two said sons to pay unto Miriam Wood my third daughter, one hundred dollars in two years after my decease.

Item, I order my son Eben to pay (when he arrives to the age of twenty one years) to my eldest son Jon a Wood forty dollars in addition to what he has already had.

Item, I order my two sons John and Eben to pay to Kimball Wood my fourth son one hundred dollars when he is twenty two years of age and one hundred dollars more when he is twenty three years of age. And I order my son Kimball to live with and work for his brothers John and Eben until he arrives to the age of nineteen years and I order them to procure and provide for him during that term sufficient meat, drink, cloathing, washing, lodging, doctoring and nursing, at their expense.

Item, I order my two sons John and Eben to pay to Jere Wood my fifth son one hundred dollars when he is twenty two years of age, and one hundred more when he is twenty three years of age.

Item, I order my two sons John and Eben to pay unto Daniel Wood, my youngest son, one hundred dollars when he is twenty two years of age, and one hundred dollars more when he is twenty three years of age.

Item, I order my two sons John and Eben to provide for their mother at my decease a decent and suitable suit of mourning and at my decease and the decease of their mother they bestow upon each of us a decent and Christian like burial and provide for each of us handsome grave stones and if any of my sons except Eben die before they be twenty one years of age his share to be equally divided between the surviving brothers.

Item, And further I hereby constitute, make and ordain Sara Wood (my beloved wife) and John Wood my second son executors of this my last will and testament be legally executed.

Item, I order my wearing apparel to be equally divided between my four oldest sons.

And I hereby utterly dissolve, revoke, and dismiss all and every former testaments, wills, and legacys, requests and executed by me in any way before this time named, willed and bequeathed, and confirming this and no other to be my last will and testament. In witness whereof I have hereunto set my hand and seal the day and year above written.

John Wood (signature)

In presence of the under written witnesses the above named John Wood signed and sealed the same to be his last will and testament,

    Roger Gilmore, Joseph Mace, Nathan Chamberlain

Helen Coll

ENOCH WELLINGTON'S ESTATE
At Probate Court for the County of Cheshire holden at Jaffrey in said county on the third day of September Anno Domino 1818.

When William Ainsworth, Esquire administrator of the estate of Enoch Wellington late of Jaffrey aforesaid deceased, made oath to the truth of the foregoing account of his administration of said estate, the same having been first examined by another subscriber Judge of the Probate estate for said county, whenceupon I do declare, that the estate aforesaid has been represented in solvent and commissioners have been appointed and impowered to receive and examine the claims of the several creditors therof according to law, who have report to me, and   ,   ,   , of all the claims which have been by them received and allowed with the particular of each claim, accounting in the whole to the sum of three hundred nineteen dollars and thirty cents. And whereas upon the settlement of the said administrator account of administration of said estate, such debts and charges as the law directs, having been first deducted, there appears to be in his hands a and remainder of the sum of four hudred and fifty dollars and ten cents. I do therefore, declare that he pay on demand being made at Jaffrey with interest after this date the advance creditors named in the list aforesaid their respective creditors named in the list aforesaid their respective claims with interest from the sixth day of February last to the date of accounting in the whole principal and interest to the sum of three hundred thirty dollars and forth fie cents. An the sum of one hundred nineteen dollars and sixty firve cents, be pay and distributed to and among the children and heirs of said deceased inequal proportions, whenever the same shall be demanded at Jaffrey aforesaid with out interest, that is to say, To Thomas Wellington, Sally, late Sally Wellington, Abigail, as Nabby Wood wife of Daniel Wood, Charlotte Wellington, Harriet Wellington, Luke Wellington, Louisa Wellington, Almira Wellington, and Sophronia Wellington, thirteen dollars twenty nine cents and four mills each.

Abel Parker, Judge of Probate

Enoch Wellington Estate
Real estate-The farm on which the deceased resided
          to be sold, or mortgage, containing 100 acres, valued at $ 1700.00
And the said Administrator pays allowance for the following charges
and payments.
Paid Jon a Wood for making coffins $ 2.75
   " Moody Lawrence for digging grave   2.75
   " Paine Wilder and Payson for funeral   2.70
   " appraisers as follows David Gilmore   1.25

Cultivating Life
A Story of Earth and Hearth

Samuel Adam 1.50 John Bemis 1.50	3.00
Notifying appraiser	2.00
Taxes paid A. Howe, Esq.	8.15
Probate fees at rendering Adm.	2.84
" " " return of inventory	1.76
" " " " of confirmation	.34
Advertising sale of estate	1.00
Spirit at vendue (vendee-to whom a thing is sold, a buyer)	4.87
paid auctioneer	1.50
My time preparing & attending vendue	2.00
paid for spirit at 2 nd. vendue	1.93
Auctioneer	1.00
my time at same & preparing	2.00
paid for showing horse before sale	.84
paid Luke Wellington for making	3.50
paid same for services after sale	4.00
paid Thomas Wellington for shelling corn	4.00
paid Levi Fisk for butter tub	.42
paid to commissioners 4 days each	12.00
spirit for comma & appraiser attending time	2.00
my time with commiss. 4 days	6.00
advertising commission	1.50
" notes of settlement	1.50
To time, trouble to amking settlements, collecting money, postage of letters or in the changes	15.00
Representation Probate	$92.60

Amt. of property sold at auction	309.25	
" sold at private sale	113.10	
" " at auction not inventoried	108.77	
" " at private sale not inventoried	9.88	
Whole amount of property		$541.20

Expenses deducted leaving a balance in the of Adm subject to the order of the court		448.60
To trouble and in paying out debts	7.25	
To probate for settlement of the amt	6.25	13.50
Balance in funds of Adm		435.10
Balance of interest		15.00
		$450.10

Helen Coll

William Ainsworth
<u>The account of William Ainsworth Administrator on the estate of Enoch Wellington late of Jaffrey</u>

First   The saide adm. charges himself with the following personal property sold at public auction by order of the court of probate
1 log chain, 1 broken chain, 1 pull chain, 1 draft chain,
1 samll iron box, 1 large iron box
1 old plow, 1 old plow, 1 new plow, 1 old wheel, 2 old wheels

cart wheels and bodies	Abijah Pierce	$16.50
1 grindstone	Laban Ripley	1.80
1 red heifer	Abel Nutting	17.10
1 brown cow	Tim R. Robinson	23.00
1 Bindle cow (dark streaks on gray)	Laban Ainsworth	23.00
1 yearling heifer	David Adams	9.25
1 " "	Paul Hunt	12.05
1 old mare	Lack Emery	11.10
1 sucking colt	David	5.00
1 bay colt	Wm. Ainsworth	60.00
1 warming oven sold to	Moody Lawrence	1.31
1 candle table	James	.40
1 pewter plate	Joel Patrick	.13
1 " "	John Wood	.14
1 " "	James	.18
1 " "	James	.21
1 " "	David Chamberlain	.12
1 " "	Luke Wellington(age 16)	.15
1 pewter platter	Parker Maynard	.37
1 " "	Matthew Hunt	.37
1 " "	Jon a Wood	.84
1 " "	Jon a Wilder	1.04
1 " "	Joel Patrick	1.46
1 dish kettle	Abel Nutting	.39
1 steel kettle	Josiah Sterns	.22
1 pudding kettle	John Turner	.56
1 pair flat irons	Jonah Cutter	.96
1 handsaw	John Ripley	.32
1 kettle	Jonas Pierce	.06
1 leather	Tim R Robinson	1.25
1 brown quilt	Wm Hodge	1.25
1 old bed quilt	Jonas Pierce	.61

Cultivating Life
A Story of Earth and Hearth

1 green quilt	Jon a Pierce	$ .92
1 " "	James	1.05
1 pair thick boots	Jonas Nutting	1.11
1 pair claf skni boots	Jon a Wood	1.80
1 old coverlet	Jonas Pierce	.43
1 sham	Jacob Baldwin	.50
1 worn coverlet	Levi Fisk	1.15
1 calico "	Abel Nutting	1.37
1 green "	John Wilder	2.61
1 blank book	Jon a Wood	1.65
1 pr. pillow cases	N. Hunt, Jr.	.18
1 "	Wm Cutter	.22
1 "	David Chamberlain	.34
1 "	Jon a Wilder	.38
1 tablecloth	Isaac Nutting	1.46
1 "	Jonas Nutting	.26
1 "	Wm Ainsworth	1.50
1 "	John Wilder	.16
1 towel	Thos. Turner	.14
1 sheet	Jonas Pierce	.85
1 "	John Wilder	.37
1 "	Thos. Turner	.46
1 "	Luke Howe	.25
1 "	Wm Cutter	.46
1 "	Jonas Nutting	.12
1 "	David Jacquith	.20
1 pine chest	Zebbidiah Pierce	1.75
1 set silver tea spoons	David Chamberlain	3.20
1 feather bed No. 3	Thos. Adam	10.12
1 trousers	N. Hunt	.18
1 spiner	Abel Nutting	1.76
1 snuff box	Luke Wellington	2.00
1 pair pantaloons	Luke Wellington	2.00
1 waistcoat	Luke Wellington	1.00
1 "	J. Sterns	1.00
1 "	Jonas Pierce	.12
1 coat	Abel Nutting	2.37
1 toast iron	Isaac Nutting	.20
1 feather bed No. 1	Jonah Cutter	13.12
1 towel	N. Hunt	.04
1 "	Thos Turner	.04

Helen Coll

1 pair pillow cases	Levi Fisk	$ .37
1 towel	Thos Turner	.17
4 "	David Chamberlain	.99
1 "	Joshus Nutting	.25
1 looking glass	Thos Tyler	1.06
1 great coat	Abel Nutting	5.00
1 almp	Thos Tyler	.23
1 sheet	Jonas Nutting	.18
1 "	Jonas Pierce	.38
1 old pillow case	Jonas Nutting	.02
1 pantaloons	Wm Ainsworth	.10
1 pair large sheetyards	Wm Ainsworth	2.60
1 pair small "	Joel Patrick	.76
1 sugar box	David Chamberlain	.11
1 glasstop bottle	David Chamberlain	.14
1 " "	N. Motts	.10
1 " "	D. Chamberlain	.18
1 kitchen chairs	Joel Patrick	<u>2.00</u>
		$297.89

Among persons on this list are: Luke Wellington, son of Enoch; sons of the next owner, Jon a Wood and John Wood; future owner Laban Ripley and his son John Ripley, future owner David Chamberlain; the father of a future owner Jonas Peirce; and neighboring farmers, Nuttings, Pierces, Cutters, and William Ainsworth, son of Rev. Laban Ainsworth.

Cultivating Life
A Story of Earth and Hearth

ESTATE OF DEXTER PIERCE

Judge of Probate   Estate of Dexter Piece
To Benjamin Pierce, Addison Pierce and Joseph Davis all of Jaffrey in said County Cheshire and Sate of New Hampshire:

You are hereby authorized to take Inventory of the Estate of Dexter Pierce late of Jaffrey in said county deceased in testate to be shown to you by May E. Pierce of said Jaffrey who has been duly appointed Administrix

October 1, 1875

Inventory of the Estate of Dexter Pierce

Real Estate		Personal Estate	
Home Farm	$1000.00	cash on hand	$ 251.00
Nutting North Lot	230.00		
	$1230.00		

Live Stock		Provisions and Produce	
3 cows	$ 75.00	6 Ton Hay	$ 70.00
2 yearlings	25.00	Corn Fodder & straw	5.00
2 calves	12.00	Lot Corn	10.00
2 pigs	6.00	38 Bush. Oats	17.00
12 turkeys	9.00	10 Bush. Apples	8.00
16 hens	4.00	50 Bus. Potatoes	10.00
	$131.00	20 lb. Butter	5.00
		Pork	1.00
		1 Bush. Beans	2.00
			$128.00

Farming Utensils & mechanics tools		Household Furniture	
1 Cart	$ 4.00	1 Cook Stove	2.00
1 Lumber Wagon	2.00	2 Stoves	4.00
1 Pleasure Wagon	5.00	1 sofa4.,lamps 1.	5.00
1 Sleigh2.00,1 Wheelbarrow2.00	4.00	6 cane chairs3.,14com.chairs	4.00
2 Harrows5.,2Plows5.	10.00	4 tables3,1	4.00
3 Hay Forks1.,2 Shovels1.	2.00	1 carpet2.,1 lounge2.	4.00
1 Harness 1.,2 Chains 1.	2.00	1 clock 1.,1 sewing machine2.	3.00
1 Drag 1., 1 Axes & hoes 2.	3.00	1 bureau1., nest tubs 1.	2.00
1 Iron Bar &Drill 1.,2 wood saws 1.	2.00	4 Beds&Bedding	16.00
1 Cross Cut Saw	1.00	crockery ware	4.00
Carpenter Tools	2.00	cutlery ware1.,tine ware2.	3.00
1 Grindstone	2.00	10 silver spoons	2.00
1 Buffalo Blanket	2.00	4 pairs 6wool Blankets	4.00
	$44.00	6 pairs cot.sheets9pillowcases	2.00

Helen Coll

<u>Misc. articles</u>   4 table covers   <u>1.00</u>
8 lb. Wool $.25   2.00 $60.00
Lot Wood in wood house   5.00
1 pair steelyards   1.00
1 set pulley blocks & rope   <u>1.00</u>
                                $9.00
Real Estate $1230.00   signed
Cash on hand   251.00   Benjamin Pierce
Live Stock   131.00   Addison Pierce
Prov.&Prod.   128.00   Joseph Davis
Farming Utensils   44.00   November 3, 1875
Household Furniture   60.00
Misc.   <u>9.00</u>
Whole Amount $1853.00

BIBLIOGRAPHY

Annett, Albert, and Alice E. E. Lehtinen. *History of Jaffrey Vol. I & II.* Peterborough, N. H.: Transcript Printing Co., 1937.

Chamberlain, Allen. *Annals of the Grand Monadnock.* Concord, N. H.: Society for the Protection of N. H. Forests, 1975.

Cutter, Daniel B. *History of Town of Jaffrey, N. H.* Concord, N. H.: Republican Press, 1881.

Wall, Steve. *Wisdom's Daughter.* N. Y.,N. Y.: Harper Perennial, 1993.

other resources:

Cheshire County Probate Court, Keene, N. H., last will and testaments, auction listings, and inventories.

Cheshire County Registry of Deeds, Keene, N. H.

Jaffrey Town Library, Jaffrey, N. H., vault reference materials.

Personal Interviews:

Thelma Jurva Lebreaux, Holden Massachusetts

Toini Jurva Palo, West Palm Beach, Florida

Norman Peard, Jaffrey, New Hampshire

Helen Coll

ABOUT THE AUTHOR

Helen Coll is a farmer, farmer's wife, mother, and businesswoman. She has lived and worked for more than forty years on their family farm in Jaffrey, New Hampshire. All of her attention for those years was on raising their children, farming the land, and building their business. A time came when she desired a change in her life and she decided to go back to college and earn her degree. This accomplishment was achieved in 1998 when she graduated from Lesley University in Cambridge, Massachusetts. From her study time she resolved to write a book about her experiences encountered in daily farm life: the family dynamics of working and living together 365 days a year; situations and conversations observed with family, business associates, customers, and employees; the pressure endured and surmounted; and the many and varied chores and workplace engagements. It was her desire to make her knowledge and experience known to a reading audience for the purpose of educating as well as entertaining them.

Printed in the United States
3830